Studying Early Printed Books 1450–1800

Studying Early Printed Books
1450–1800

A Practical Guide

Sarah Werner

WILEY Blackwell

Registered Offices
John Wiley & Sons, Inc., 111 River Street, Hoboken, NJ 07030, USA
John Wiley & Sons Ltd, The Atrium, Southern Gate, Chichester, West Sussex, PO19 8SQ, UK

Editorial Office
The Atrium, Southern Gate, Chichester, West Sussex, PO19 8SQ, UK

For details of our global editorial offices, customer services, and more information about
Wiley products visit us at www.wiley.com.

Wiley also publishes its books in a variety of electronic formats and by print-on-demand.
Some content that appears in standard print versions of this book may not be available in
other formats.

Library of Congress Cataloging-in-Publication data applied for

Hardback ISBN: 9781119049975
Paperback ISBN: 9781119049968

Cover images: 1) Side view of a printing press from the 1769 *Encyclopédie*, from a public
domain image made available by Smithsonian Libraries; 2) A blank leaf from Donne's
1633 *Juvenilia*, provided by the Folger Shakespeare Library under a CC BY-SA license.
Cover design: Wiley

Set in 10/12pt Warnock by SPi Global, Pondicherry, India

Contents

List of Illustrations

Acknowledgments

This book has been long in the making and my debts of gratitude are many. Deep thanks go to Adam Hooks and Dan Traister, who read the manuscript in full and provided many helpful comments throughout; this book is stronger for their generosity. I am thankful, too, for the advice of others who have read small and large chunks of this: Jason Dean, Sophie Defrance, Marieke van Delft, Rachel Donohue, Ian Gadd, Erik Geleijns, Shanti Graheli, Daryl Green, Whitney Trettien, and Steven Van Impe. A number of folks helped me track down resources and answer questions: thank you, Giles Bergel, Thony Christie, Heather Froelich, John Gallagher, Marian Lefferts, and Aaron Pratt. As I wrote this, I chatted about it a lot, particularly on Twitter, where I have found a community who help me think about the production and use of rare materials; so for assistance in pinning down details and for getting excited about the big picture, thank you #biblionerds, especially Mitch Fraas, Bob MacLean, Jay Moschella, John Overholt, and Shannon Supple. The cheering on of my friends, and their willingness to listen to me despair, kept me going (hi, snails and shoal). And my family learned more than they probably wanted to about all of this and they usually listened to my explaining all the ups and downs.

The origins of the idea for this book came from a long-ago conversation with Emma Bennett, then acquisition editor at Wiley Blackwell, and her excitement for this persuaded me it was doable. I am grateful to her, Deirdre Illkson, and Rebecca Harkin for their conversations and support. Manish Luthra shepherded this book through production, copy editor Giles Flitney brought clarity to my thoughts, and Juliet Booker provided invaluable help in making the book look its best.

The images in this book come from libraries that provide high-resolution and open-access images of their collections. Not all institutions use public domain or share-alike licensing, but it's not only the legal choice, it's the right choice: we are custodians of these objects not for our own benefit but for everyone's. Thank you, Boston Public Library, Folger Shakespeare Library, Harry Ransom Center, Library of Congress, Metropolitan Museum of Art, National Library of Medicine, Smithsonian Libraries, the University and State Library of Cologne, and the University of Ghent Library.

But my two largest debts of gratitude are to people without whom I would not have been able to even think about the questions that this book asks, let alone begin to explain how to answer them. My former colleagues in the Folger Shakespeare Library's Central Library are a font of wisdom and generosity. I have learned more than I can express not only from their conversations with me but from their catalog and acquisitions records and conservation work and reading guidelines—in other words, from all aspects of the work they do, too often unrecognized, every day. Thank you Julie Ainsworth, Ron Bogdan, Erin Blake, Melissa Cook, William Davis, LuEllen DeHaven, Rhea DeStefano, Steve Galbraith, Jim Kuhn, Rosalind Larry, Caryn Lazzuri, Deborah Leslie, Renate Mesmer, Camille Seerattan, Carrie Smith, Heather Wolfe, and Georgianna Ziegler, and my thanks to Nadia Seiler and Betsy Walsh, may their memories be a blessing.

Finally, it is to the students I taught in the Folger Undergraduate Program's "Books and Early Modern Culture" seminar that I owe my biggest debt of gratitude. Their enthusiasm for and openness to working with all aspects of bibliography and book history drove me to learn more and share more with them. We asked questions together and learned together. It's in their honor that I hope this book inspires more people to look at their books with open eyes and open hearts.

Introduction

If you buy a book today at your local book store and enjoy it so much you want to share it with your globe-trotting Aunt Sadie, you'd expect that the copy you buy online and have shipped to her will be the same book that you own. It'd have the same cover, the same number of pages, the same text on all those pages. But if you lived in 1573, and you bought a book at a bookstall near St Paul's Cathedral in London, and then met up to discuss that book with a friend who had also bought a copy at the same stall, you might discover that your books looked very different. They might have different bindings, they might have different words on some of the pages, they might even not have the same number of leaves.

That difference between books then and books today is why this book exists. Everything that we assume about print today—that it is fixed, easily replicated, identical in mass quantities—are features that were gradually established during the first centuries of printing. In order to understand what an early modern book is and how printed conventions came to be what they are, we need to understand how early printed books were made. And so this guide describes the technologies and practices of hand-press printing in order to help us identify how the mechanics of making books shapes how we read and understand them.

When Johannes Gutenberg created movable type and the printing press in the late 1440s and early 1450s, he was drawing on existing practices and technologies in metalworking and wine making and tapping into an established market for manuscript books and for woodcut prints. What Gutenberg set into motion was the ability to create a large variety of texts printed in large quantities; a 400-page work didn't need 400 different woodblocks to print it, but a font of type that could be arranged into different words and rearranged into different words for corrections and other books.

Studying Early Printed Books 1450–1800: A Practical Guide, First Edition. Sarah Werner.
© 2019 Sarah Werner. Published 2019 by John Wiley & Sons Ltd.

The technologies associated with Gutenberg—type cast from metal matrices, wooden press operated by hand, and black ink from oil and soot—remained largely the same until machines were introduced to the process in the early 1800s. The practices of how books were made and how they were sold changed over time, especially in the first 50 years of printing when many of the conventions we take for granted, like title pages, were still being developed. But how type was cast and books were printed remained essentially consistent until machines entered the picture. And so, although the period of hand-press printing in the West stretches over 250 years and across Europe and North America, we can study its practices as a rough continuum. What you learn about how a book was printed in Leipzig in 1502 will be relevant for a pamphlet printed in Boston in 1784.

The focus of this guide is on printed works, but the distinction between print and manuscript is less strict than we have come to assume today. The development of the printing press happened alongside a growth in manuscript production; the increased availability of paper made both printing and writing on paper easier. The earliest printed books often depended on manuscript completion; the addition of initial letters and rubrication to mark the start of passages blur the line between printed books and hand-written ones. Even later printed books worked hand in hand with manuscript practices, encouraging readers to write in corrections for print errors and users to copy out printed passages in their manuscript miscellanies (compilations of miscellaneous texts). The rise of print also meant an increase in printed forms designed to be completed by hand; indeed the earliest surviving printed works were not books but indulgences with blank spaces left for the purchaser's name. David McKitterick's *Print, Manuscript, and the Search for Order, 1450-1830* provides illuminating details and a historical framework for understanding why print and manuscript should be considered alongside each other. But an introductory book can only cover so much material. Since more readers encounter early modern works in their printed form, rather than in manuscript, and since reading early modern handwriting is a skill unto itself, this guide keeps its focus on understanding printed books. (If you're interested in learning more about early modern manuscripts and paleography, see Appendix 1, "Further Reading," for some resources.)

If print and manuscript are blurred categories, so is that of books. We tend to think of printing as making books and of books as printed objects. But there are plenty of printed works that are not in the form of a codex (the technical term for a gathering of leaves secured along one side—that is, the form of the book as we are used to it). Forms, pamphlets, playbills, proclamations, and news sheets are examples of early printed objects that are not books, but that are an integral part of the print trade. And there are plenty of codices that are not printed, in medieval and earlier periods and continuing through the early modern and modern periods. Manuscript bibles, books of poems, account books, miscellanies, and diaries are usually in the form of a codex. For simplicity's sake, this guide describes our object of study as printed books, but the printing processes discussed here are true for any printed work in the hand-press period, codex or not.

It's also important to remember from the outset that we base our knowledge of early printed books on what has survived, but those survivors aren't necessarily representative of what was being printed and read. Collectors have long had a bias toward books they deemed important and so literary works were saved at a much greater rate than almanacs. Some printed works were built for survival—those heavy bound bibles. Others were barely intended to last through the week—printed broadsides pasted to walls would disappear as soon as it rained, if not before. We work with what we have, but we can try to remember there's a lot we don't have. (For more on what survived and what's missing, see "Loss Rates" in Part 5.)

But why do you need to know how hand-press books are made or how to read them? Can't you just pick up an edition of *Utopia* and be done with it? You certainly could. There are plenty of modern editions not only of *Utopia* but of many of Thomas More's other works as well. But an interest in *Utopia* can easily lead to an interest in the humanist circles through which it moved and the various letters and poems and other material that preceded and followed early editions of the book. Such paratextual material, however, is usually appended to the end of a modern edition, if it's included at all, while the early editions published some material before the main text and some after, and the first four Latin editions varied in what material was included and where it appeared. In other words, modern editions of this text don't include all the information that an early reader would have seen and a modern researcher might want. And, of course, many other early printed books don't exist in any modern edition.

There's also information to be found in looking at a book's original printing that can help us understand how it was used. Take a look at the title page in Figure 1, for example.

•

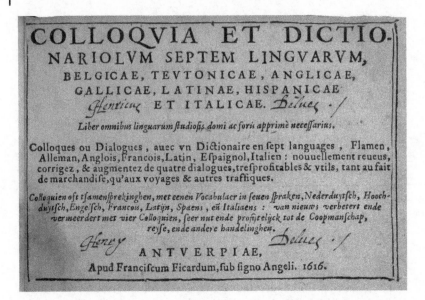

Figure 1 The title page to a 1616 edition of *Colloquia et dictionariolum septem linguarum,* often referred to as a Berlaimont (or Berlemont) after the original traveler's vocabularies created by Noël de Berlaimont. Image made available by the Folger Shakespeare Library under a CC BY-SA 4.0 license (STC 1431.86).

What strikes you about it? One of the questions you might ask—though it's easier to notice when you're holding it in your hand, rather than looking at a picture—is why it's shaped so oddly. Books generally are vertical rectangles, taller than they are wide. This title page, however, is decidedly squat, perhaps one-and-a-half times as wide as it is tall. Why does it look like this? And why is the title page so dense? You might also notice that there are three blocks of text on the page, rather than a clearly identified title and author as is usual today.

If you could hold it in your hand, you would see that it's in an old leather binding with what look like broken clasps attached. The first couple of leaves of the book come before the title page and have hand-written notes on them, as do the last leaves of the book. And the printed text, which makes up the bulk of the 400 or so pages of the volume, is made up of seven columns of text in varying styles of print.

It's a funny, repetitive little book, at first glance. But why is it so? If you can read the Latin, French, or Dutch on the title page, you will have already started to work out what this book is: it's a dictionary with dialogues and vocabulary lists in seven languages. It's squat in part because it has to fit seven columns of text across the page openings, one each for Flemish, German, English, French, Latin, Spanish, and Italian. It's also squat because it's meant to be a size you can easily carry with you and refer to as needed; that's in part why it has clasps across the fore-edge, to keep it closed and secure from damage when being carried. Imagine reading this in a modern edition (were a modern edition to exist): Would it be the same if it was shaped like our books usually are?

This Berlaimont (so-called because the first of its type was created by a schoolmaster named Noël de Berlaimont [or Berlemont] in the 1520s) offers all sorts of information to those willing to look. How do you make a book this shape? What's the audience for it? What were the geographies and politics of the 16th through the 18th centuries that created such a demand that it continued to be expanded and reprinted for all that time? What sort of cultural values could we learn from reading these everyday dialogues?

But first you need to learn that these are questions you can and should ask. You need to understand how early printed books are made and that their making shapes their use and our study of them. That's where this book comes in.

The aim of this guide is to show you how to think about the connections between the material form of a book (what it looks like and how it was made) and how that book conveys its meaning and how it is used by readers. The questions that we just asked of the Berlaimont—about how it was made and what its effect is on users—are questions that bibliographers ask. Up to this point, you might have thought of bibliography as the making of lists of books; it's what you are taught to do as students, and it's an important aspect of research. But bibliography can also be the study of how books are made, and that's our focus here. That study, I think, can be the most compelling when it is connected to how books are used—how people handled them, how they were marketed, how they were read, how they were shared and shaped by the people who owned them. That is why I try to ask throughout this book how aspects of a book's making can shape our understanding of it.

This focus on bibliography is also why I refer to a book's users rather than to its readers. Books are certainly read, but there are many types of reading—browsing, memorizing, reading for pleasure, reading for work. And there are many things you can do with books other than read them—you can write in them, take them apart, display them, share them, and throw them away. All of these uses are part of how we experience books and part of what we should consider when we study them. The way a book is made shapes how it is used and how it gets passed down to us. To think like a bibliographer is to notice a book's features and to ask how and why. And it is, I hope, a way of valuing books and being excited to work with them.

Studying Early Printed Books 1450–1800: A Practical Guide is divided into parts that can be read sequentially or not, depending on your needs. Part 1, "Overview," takes you through the steps of making a book from a stack of plain paper through a (maybe, maybe not!) bound book. If this is your first time learning about hand-press books, you will want to start here. Part 2, "Step-by-Step," is a closer look at the different processes that together make a book. It's divided into discrete sections that roughly follow the order of book making. "Paper" therefore comes before "Printing," and "Binding" comes at the end. Each of these sections concludes with a piece on "Why does it matter?" which seeks to give examples of how understanding these processes can help us study early printed books. You might not need to read all of these sections in depth—perhaps you don't need to learn about the entire process of making paper, but you do need a more detailed account of formats. You can jump back and forth between Part 1 and Part 2, or you can read 1 first and then 2, but not all of the overview that is provided in 1 is in 2. It might be best to think of 1 and 2 as making up a spiral in which 2 circles back to material introduced in 1 and covers it in greater detail. Part 3, "On the Page," examines some of the typographic elements you'll see on early printed pages. If you're confused about the purpose of signature marks or curious about different types of title pages, this is where you'll find out more.

Although this whole guide is designed to be used alongside reading early printed books, the next two parts focus explicitly on a plan of action for using early books. Part 4, "Looking at Books," explains how you can learn to look at a book in order to see the clues it offers about its making and use. Organized around a series of questions to prompt your examination, it will start to train you to act as a bibliographer, looking at material evidence and drawing conclusions about what it means. Part 5, "The Afterlives of Books," helps you differentiate between early modern elements and the parts of books that have been subsequently altered. Any book that you see today, whether in person in a library or on your computer screen at home, has passed through multiple hands to get to you, and in that passage of time, it has been altered. Part 5 will take you through the process of thinking about a book as a time capsule and considers the value of studying it as such.

Studying Early Printed Books concludes with two appendices. The first provides a list of accessible readings that can help you continue your bibliographic studies; any works I refer to in the course of the book are included there, as well as additional readings that can guide your further research. It's not an exhaustive list, but one focused on works that are significant to the field and engaging for beginners to it. It's organized by topic, roughly in the order in which the book addresses them, so that you can quickly find additional information on the subject you're curious about. Any works that I cite will be in this appendix; in many regards, this guide serves as an introduction to Philip Gaskell's *A New Introduction to Bibliography*, and if you are curious to learn more about how hand-press books were made, that is the best source to turn to next. When I am discussing examples of hand-press books, those are given a standard bibliographic citation—like STC 22273 or EDIT16 26111—so that you can look them up; a list and description of those references is in the appendix as well, in the section on catalogs.

The second appendix is a glossary of terms that I and other bibliographers use frequently, gathered together for quick reference. While I define such terms the first time I use them, the glossary will be a resource for you when you encounter bibliographic language not only here but in your further research.

I have tried to include helpful illustrations throughout the book, especially in the first parts. But you can best learn about books by looking at plenty of examples. If you have access to a nearby library that collects rare books, you should visit it regularly and explore its holdings. If finding hand-press books is hard to do, or if you're curious to see further examples and resources, you might wish to browse the accompanying website, Early Printed Books (http://www.earlyprintedbooks.com).

A note about gender

I'm primarily using "he" as a pronoun for printers because the book trade in the hand-press period was overwhelmingly male. But I also use the occasional "she" because there certainly were women working in the printing trades, as publishers and as printers. The work of Helen Smith and others helps to illuminate their too-often hidden presence in printing history.

Part 1
Overview

The process of making a book is the transformation of blank sheets of paper into sequential pages of printed text. It's a process that moves through many steps, the details of which shape not only the final object but its distribution and use.

This part of the guide will provide an overview of printing a book, first describing the processes of making a book and then considering some of their consequences for the economics of book production. The second part of this guide will give more detailed information on these processes; readers might wish to read both parts simultaneously, moving from overview to detail as needed, or to read the overview and then proceed to details. I explain the technical terms being used as they come up, but there is also a glossary in Appendix 2 that will be of assistance.

A note about roles

The terms that we use today to think of the different roles in making books are not the terms that were used in the hand-press period. "Printer" referred to the person whose business was to operate the printing press. But a "printer" could also be the person who caused the book to come into print and who supplied the money for the venture, a role that today we would identify as the publisher. The person doing the printing might or might not have been the same person acting as publisher. (The demarcation between those roles changed over the hand-press period, with publishers gradually differentiating themselves from printers and becoming wealthier and more dominant in the trade.) The third step in the process—getting the book into the hands of readers—was handled by booksellers, who may or may not also have been publishers. Although "publisher" is not a term contemporary with the period, it is a helpful way of understanding the different functions in making and selling books.

Getting Ready to Print

The first step in printing an early modern book—assuming you have something you want to print—starts with a pile of blank paper.

Studying Early Printed Books 1450–1800: A Practical Guide, First Edition. Sarah Werner.
© 2019 Sarah Werner. Published 2019 by John Wiley & Sons Ltd.

(Technically, it starts with the stuff that makes paper; for more on that, see "Paper" in Part 2.) Paper was usually the responsibility of the person paying for the book to be printed, not the person printing the book. Given the sheer volume of paper needed to print a book, it was easily the most expensive element of making one—nearly half the cost. Although individual sheets of paper weren't necessarily expensive, even a small print run of a small book meant thousands of sheets of paper, and so the cost rapidly added up.

The printer's responsibility was turning those blank sheets into a sequentially ordered text. In hand-press printing, and in machine printing, sheets of paper are printed with multiple pages of text; after both sides of a sheet are printed, folded, gathered, and cut open, the resulting leaves can be read in order. Figures 2–4 provide a quick illustration. Take a sheet of paper and fold it once in half: now you have a sheet that's been divided into two leaves, or four pages; we would call this format a folio. Fold that sheet of paper again: now your sheet has been turned into four leaves, or eight pages; this is a quarto.

Printing on vellum

Although hand-press books were overwhelmingly printed on paper, some early books were printed on parchment (sheep skin) or vellum (calf skin). But the cost of procuring enough skin to print even small print runs of books was expensive. And vellum, which shrank and expanded depending on humidity, was not ideally suited for working with presses.

If you number the pages 1 through 8, and then unfold your booklet, you'll see how a text would need to be imposed, or laid out on the sheet of paper in order to make sense when it is folded. That is how a printer would want to lay out the type to be printed, with multiple pages for one sheet. ("Format" in Part 2 provides a more detailed explanation of the concepts of imposition and format.)

If you look at your unfolded quarto, you'll see that pages 1, 4, 5, and 8 are on one side of the sheet of paper, and pages 2, 3, 6, and 7 are on the other side. You could, if you were a printer working from a manuscript, set the first page in type, then the second page, then the third, on through the eighth, and then print the first side of the sheet and then the second. (Indeed, setting serially like this was one way printers worked.) But proceeding this way would mean that the press is sitting idle while the entire booklet is being set. A more efficient operation (albeit a confusing one to the uninitiated) would be to print by forme: the first side of the sheet is printed while the second side is being set.

The trick to this, however, is that the printer needs to know where the fourth page starts even though the second and third pages haven't yet

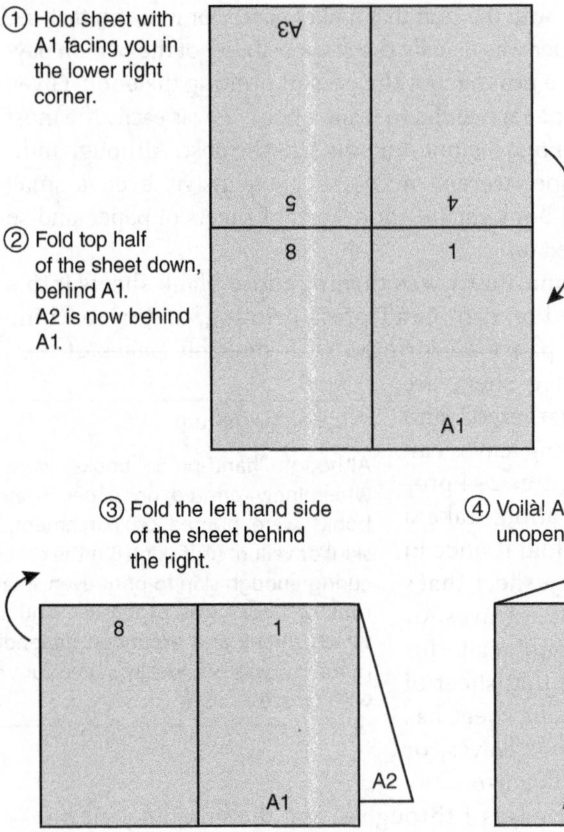

① Hold sheet with A1 facing you in the lower right corner.

② Fold top half of the sheet down, behind A1. A2 is now behind A1.

③ Fold the left hand side of the sheet behind the right.

④ Voilà! An unopened quarto!

Figures 2–4 How a sheet of paper turns into eight pages. Based on a sketch by the author.

been set in type. And so, even before the type for the first page is set, someone in the print shop needs to read through the manuscript, marking off where each page starts so that the person setting the type (the compositor) knows where to start and stop each page. This process, called casting off, requires knowing what size the pages will be and a sense of the book's typography (e.g. what size type will be used, how many illustrations, whether the book is in prose or verse), factors that will affect how many lines fit on a page and how much text fits on each line. But an experienced compositor will be able to estimate how much manuscript text will convert to a printed page so that setting the type will usually proceed smoothly.

Once the compositors know what they're working from, and where the pages of set type start and stop, the work of transforming the text into print begins.

A compositor works standing in front of a single or pair of type cases with the text he's working from hanging in front of him. Each case has compartments, one for each sort (letter, punctuation, or space), with larger compartments for the more frequently used characters and smaller compartments for those used less frequently. For instance, if you look at the illustration in Figure 5 from Joseph Moxon's 1683 *Mechanick Exercises: or, the doctrine of handy-works. Applied to the art of Printing* (Wing

Where does the text come from?

Nearly anywhere! A text could be supplied by its author, by a publisher, by a third party who might or might not have been authorized by the author to share it; it could be newly written, an edition or translation of an already existing work, or nearly any other permutation. The text the compositors set from (known as the "copy text") could be in manuscript, in print, or in print marked up with manuscript annotations. For our purposes, the source of the text doesn't matter, since the process it will go through in being printed will be the same regardless.

M3014), you'll see that the letter "e" has a huge compartment, while "x" has a small one; "e" is the most frequently used letter in English, while "x" is of course used only rarely.

You'll also notice in looking at Moxon that two boxes below the "e" is a box marked with what we think of as a hash mark. In typography, # is used to indicate a space (proofreaders still use the symbol this way in correcting text). In this diagram, the box marked with # is the box

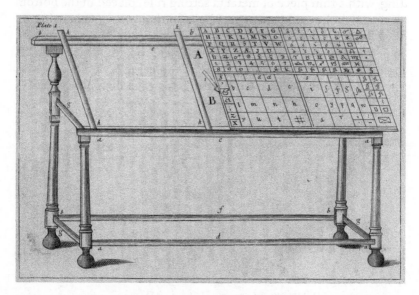

Figure 5 A pair of type cases from Moxon's 1683 *Mechanick Exercises: or, the doctrine of handy-works. Applied to the art of Printing* (Wing M3014). Public domain image made available by the Boston Public Library (G.676.M87R v.2, plate 1).

storing the spaces. We might not think of spaces as pieces of type, since the point of a space is that it doesn't leave a mark, but letterpress printing requires the surface of what's to be printed to be absolutely steady—any wobbling or moving about will mean that the type won't print clearly. And so the entire text area needs to be firmly locked into place, with no gaps even where the white spaces are. If the sentence you are now reading were to have been set in type in the hand-press era, it would have consisted of 145 separate pieces of metal. There would be 112 individual letters, 3 numbers, 3 pieces of punctuation, and 27 spaces to be picked out of the type case to form that sentence.

That count assumes that every letter in that sentence is a piece of type. But just as it's important to remember that spaces are pieces of type, we need to remember that a piece of type might be made up of multiple letters. On the far right of the lower case in Moxon's diagram are compartments for ligatures, letters that are joined together to form one piece of type. The most common ligatures in English involved the long-s (ſ) and f, letters that curved over at the top and that would hit the adjacent letter if it had a tall ascender. And so ſl, ſh, ff, fl, and ff are each made as single sorts, rather than two sorts placed next to each other. (See "Type" in Part 2 for more information on how type is made.)

Standing in front of the type cases, a compositor holds in his left hand a composing stick adjusted to the width of the text he is setting, with a thin piece of metal (a setting rule) placed in the bottom of the stick. Looking at the text he is setting, which is hanging on the type cases, he chooses each piece of type, one by one, from the appropriate box and places it in the composing stick with his right hand. Since the arrangement of the cases is familiar to him, the compositor doesn't need to search for each box, but rather his

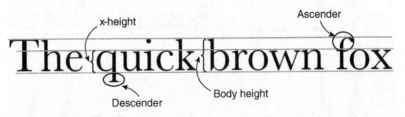

Figure 6 The basic parts of letters. Illustration by the author.

hand can quickly go to where it is needed. (Think about touch typing and how adept typists don't need to look at their fingers in order to be able to type out their text, or about how fluent pianists know where the keys are.) Each piece of metal type has near its base an indentation, or nick, to indicate its correct orientation: if all the nicks are aligned, then all of the letters, numbers, or symbols will be facing the correct direction. The face of the piece of type (where the letter is) would be immediately differentiated from its base by touch as well, since it would have the raised letter on it. Spaces would have blank faces and they would be a bit shorter than those with characters, since you wouldn't want them to be inked and accidentally print marks.

Starting on the left side of the stick, the compositor uses his thumb to keep the sorts in place as the line gets filled out. Once the type fills out the pre-measured line, the compositor adjusts the type so that it fits tightly, perhaps filling out the line with additional spaces, hyphenating a word so that it's split between two lines, using an abbreviation, or adjusting the spelling of a word so that the line is fully justified. (Text is described as justified when it is evenly lined up against the margin; the text in this book is fully justified and even on both sides, but text can also be set so that it's justified on one side and ragged on the other.) Some composing sticks, like those typically used by the French, held only one line of type at a time; English sticks, however, were deep enough that multiple lines of text could be set in the stick. In those cases, after the first line of type is justified, the compositor slides the setting rule out of the bottom of the stick and places it on top of the line of set type so that it provides a smooth surface for the pieces of type to move along; he then proceeds to set the next line of text in the same fashion. Since the type is set upside down, reading from left to right, and with the tops of the characters at the bottom of the stick (see Figure 7), subsequent lines of type can appear on top of the first line. (Of course, the letters themselves are also reversed, like rubber stamps: the letters on the face of the stamp are their mirror image, so that the inked paper reads in the correct orientation.)

A note about leading

Sometimes a book's typography would call for the space between lines of type to be larger than the sorts themselves provide. In these situations, a compositor would insert strips of metal between the lines of type in order to increase the white space between them, a feature known as leading (pronounced to rhyme with "wedding"), presumably after the metal used for the strips. Such leading could happen in the composing stick, or after the type had been transferred to the galley. English books were not typically leaded before the 18th century.

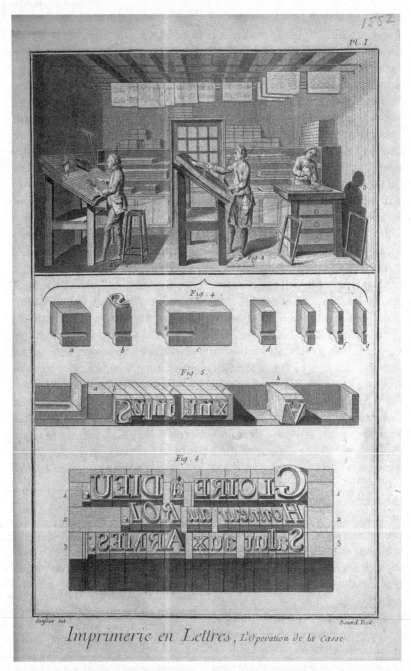

Figure 7 Compositors and composing sticks from the 1769 *Encyclopédie ou Dictionnaire raisonné des sciences, des arts et des métiers*. The pieces of type show the nicks near the bottom are all facing the same way, so that the faces of the letters are oriented correctly. Public domain image made available by the Smithsonian Libraries (AE25.E53X 1751 Plates, t. 7, "Imprimerie en caracteres," plate 1).

Once the composing stick is full, the type needs to be transferred to a galley (a two- or three-sided wooden tray about the size of a page) so that the stick is free for setting more type. Using the setting rule and his thumbs to squeeze the type together so that the pieces stay in order, the compositor slides the set type off the stick onto a galley, where it can wait until the remainder of the page has been set. If there are multiple lines of type in the stick, the whole group can be slid off together and oriented on the gallery accordingly.

After the compositor has finished setting the page's text, he'll mark his spot in the text he's working from and tie up the type with twine so that the pieces stay in order. After tying it off, he slides the set page off the galley, perhaps wrapping it in paper if it's going to be sitting a while, and moves on to setting the next page. The compositor will continue following the same process until the entire side of the sheet is done. One thing to note is that the compositor is often responsible for details like what woodcuts are used for initial letters and head-pieces (see in Part 3 "Initial Letters" and "Printer's Ornaments"). He was also usually responsible for spelling and punctuation. Although occasionally authors were involved in the printing process and insisted on particular details, typically a compositor spelled words according to his custom, not as they were spelled in the copy text.

If the book being printed is in quarto format, with four leaves and therefore four pages to a side of a sheet of paper, all four pages will be transferred to an imposing stone where they can be arranged in order within the chase (an iron frame that will keep the type in place). Using the direction lines, the compositor identifies which pages go where so that they'll print in the correct sequence. (A direction line is the text at the bottom of the page that identifies where a page goes through signature marks and catchwords.) The next step, if this is one of the early formes printed for a book, is to set the headlines (the information at the very top of the page, usually including the work or section title and its page or leaf number, as you can see at the top of this page).

Finally, once all of the text is set, the whole forme is locked into place so that there are no loose pieces. Wooden sticks (furniture) and wedges (quoins) are used to fill out the gaps between the type-set page and the frame of the chase. All of the empty space in the chase need not be filled, but

Leaves and pages

Today we think of books in terms of pages—each piece of paper has two sides, and those pages are numbered, or paginated. But early books were sometimes counted in terms of leaves—that is, the piece of paper is numbered, not the pages. Those books are referred to as being foliated, rather than paginated.

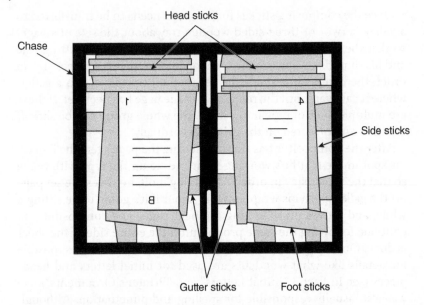

Figure 8 A locked chase, showing the furniture and quoins holding a folio imposition in place. Based on a sketch by the author.

there needs to be enough pressure exerted on the type that it doesn't shift—any looseness will mean that when the chase is picked up to carry to the press, the type will pie (spill out of position). But once the forme is locked in place, it's ready to be printed.

At the Press

With the forme set and locked, the chase is carried to the press and placed on the press stone. One of the two pressmen working the press adjusts the forme so that the printed sheets will register correctly, that is, each inked forme lining up squarely with the sheet of paper and, if it's the second side of a sheet, lining up with what's already been printed.

The pressman also needs to pack the tympan, if it's the first print job of the day, and make the frisket frame. The tympan is the part of the press that holds the paper (see Figure 9). Because the pressure of the press forces the type into the paper, the tympan is packed with a woolen blanket to absorb some of the bite, allowing any slightly uneven type to make clean impressions and preventing the type from tearing the paper.

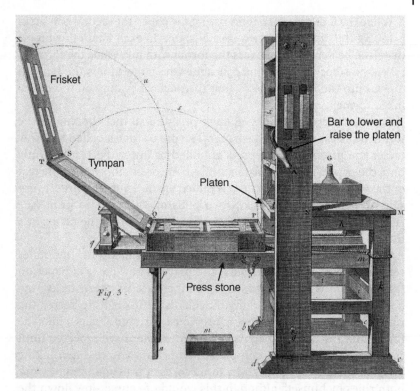

Figure 9 Side view of a printing press, labeled with key parts; adapted from a public domain image from the *Encyclopédie* made available by Smithsonian Libraries (AE25.E53X 1751 Plates, t.7, "Imprimerie en caracteres," plate 15).

The frisket serves two purposes: it helps hold the paper onto the tympan, and it masks off the parts of the paper that are not to be printed, such as white areas or text that will be printed a different color (see "Printing" in Part 2 for details about two-color printing). In order to make the masking frame, the pressman lays a sheet of parchment on the tympan, pulls an impression of the forme, and then cuts away the printed areas. The resulting frame is then attached to the frisket.

The paper, meanwhile, has been dampened and flattened overnight so that it is ready to take the ink smoothly. The pressman takes a sheet of paper from the pile next to him and places it on the tympan, piercing it with the points and closing the frisket on top of it. The points are small, sharp pieces of metal on the tympan frame; the points pierce the paper and help hold it in place, and the resulting point holes orient the paper correctly when the second side is printed.

While the first pressman is preparing the paper, the second pressman is inking the type. Using two ink balls, one in each hand, this press-man (the beater) evenly covers the forme with ink. Once the forme is inked, he steps back and his colleague (the puller) folds the tympan down onto the press stone so that the paper is resting on top of the inked forme.

The next step is to apply enough pressure so that the ink on the forme transfers evenly to the paper. The press stone is rolled half-way under the platen and the press is pulled to lower the platen firmly onto the paper. Then the platen is lifted, the press stone rolled the rest of the way under, and the press is pulled again. In other words, every side of a sheet of paper takes two pulls on the press to print (see "Printing" in Part 2 for why only half a sheet is under the platen at a time).

With the forme fully printed, the stone is rolled out, the puller removes the paper, puts it aside, and places a new piece of paper on the tympan. While the puller is taking care of these tasks, the beater—who has been working the ink on the ink balls to keep it the right consistency and reviewing previously printed sheets—inks the forme and the process begins again. These steps are repeated until the entire run has been completed, with the two pressmen taking turns in the different roles. (In some cases, a pressman might work both roles by himself, although this would of course slow down the rate of production. Some pressmen also employed boys, known as printers' devils, to take the printed sheets off the press, thereby speeding up their rate of work.)

While one forme is being run through the press, the next forme is being worked on by the compositors, each page being set in type and then the necessary pages locked up in the chase as described before. When all the required sheets of the first forme are done, the forme is removed from the press stone and replaced with the next one.

How fast did they work?

Surviving evidence about the rate at which printers worked shows a wide range of how many sheets they printed a day. Records of output and contracts for wages range from around 1,550 impressions a day to 3,450 impressions a day. (An impression accounts for one pass through the press, so generally one side of a sheet.) It's probably safe to assume an average of 2,500 impressions a day, although you should keep in mind that early modern printers generally worked much longer hours than we tend to—at least 12 hours a day, six days a week, about double our standard work week. (See Gaskell's sections on "output," especially pp. 139–141, for further detail and source material.)

Also at the Press

For the sake of continuity, this description of printing took us straight through from putting the chase on the stone through printing the last sheet of that forme. But the printing process didn't always proceed without interruption. One of the great advantages of movable type is that it could be moved: it could be set and then any portion of it changed. One result of this is that printers could run proof sheets and correct errors before printing the entire run of a forme. A printer would print off a single copy of a forme and have it examined for mistakes or other necessary changes. Corrections were marked on the proof sheet using a set of symbols that are much like the symbols that proofreaders today use. If there were changes that needed to be made, the compositor would unlock the forme, pick out the offending type, and replace it with the correction. Depending on how much was removed and what it was replaced with, there might only be one line that would have to be adjusted and justified, or multiple lines. Since the page still needed to end in the same spot (if it didn't, it would really disrupt the printing process), the compositor would strive to adjust spelling and spacing to ensure that the new type fit into the space that was allotted for the old type. Once corrected, the forme would be locked up again and ready to print.

A note about corrections

Given the difficulty of picking out type and replacing it with different type, sometimes the process of changing introduced new errors rather than only fixing old errors. It's also not always clear from extant copies which state might have been the "uncorrected" state and which the "corrected." For both of these reasons, it's more accurate to refer to stop-press changes rather than stop-press corrections. (See "Corrections" in Part 2 for more on how printers made changes to the printed text.)

Proofing generally happened before a print run got underway. But at any point in the process, printing could be interrupted and changes made. In these instances, the printing would halt, the changes would be made to the type on the stone, and then the forme would be locked up again and the printing continue. But the first part of the print run—the sheets that were printed before the changes were made—would not be corrected or discarded because paper was too expensive to waste for small errors. The end result could be 300 sheets in the first state (A) and 200 sheets in the second state (B). Flip those sheets over to print the second forme, possibly again with a first state (X) and a second state (Y), and you could end up with 500 sheets in different combinations of A/X, B/X, A/Y, and B/Y. And when those books are sold, there's no indication of which sheets are which and what's in the book you buy; you and your friend could each buy a copy of the same book from the same bookseller at the same time, and still end up with copies that differ from each other.

After Printing

After being removed from the press stone, the finished forme is scrubbed clean of ink. If the type is not immediately needed, the pages of type might remain tied up and set aside, but leaving type standing for any length of time is unusual in the hand-press period. (Type was expensive and printers might not keep more than about eight sheets worth of type on hand. Leaving type standing meant that it was unavailable to be used for other sheets, thereby limiting an already limited resource.)

The process of returning type to its case is known as distributing type. After unlocking the cleaned forme from the chase so that the type can be removed, the compositor will pick up a few lines of type with his left hand, carry them over to his case, and with his right hand, pick up individual pieces of type and return them to the appropriate box. The trick, of course, is that he needs to identify what the type is even as the letterform on its face is reversed (remember, type is the mirror of how letters appear when printed) and he needs to drop the letter in its correct box. If a piece of type is returned to the wrong box, it could remain with those sorts and possibly be used in place of one of the correct pieces of type the next time type is set.

The aim of this process is not to create an entirely clean stone on which the next forme can be set, however. It's to create an empty space into which the elements of a forme that change can be replaced. Since the pages of a book can be expected to all have the same-sized area of printed text and of white space, it is logical that the furniture and quoins that were used to lock one forme up can be reused to lock up other formes for the same book. Rather than having to hunt anew for the right combination of material to keep the type firmly in place, the furniture and quoins from one forme will be left for the next.

The same principle is true of the headlines—the lines of text at the top of each page identifying the book and, sometimes, the pagination or foliation. Since the title of the book tends to remain consistent (even headlines that identify the section of a work rather than the

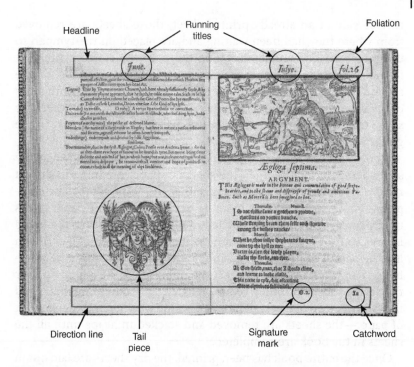

Headline

Running titles

Foliation

Direction line

Tail piece

Signature mark

Catchword

Figure 10 An opening from Spenser's 1579 poem *The shepheardes calender* (STC 23089) labeled with some standard page elements. Labels added to an image made available by the Folger Shakespeare Library under a CC BY-SA 4.0 license (STC 23089, sigs. G1v-G2r).

overall title tend to repeat over multiple sheets), it makes sense to leave the headlines on the imposing stone rather than distributing their type.

These elements that are reused from one forme to the next are known as the skeleton of a forme; they are the structural foundation that remains behind after the other parts are stripped away.

When it is time to set the new forme, the compositor places the pages of set type as appropriate within the chase, and the skeleton's foliation or pagination numbers are adjusted as needed. The gutter sticks, head sticks, and other furniture and quoins are then placed inside the chase to lock everything up firmly, and then the forme is ready to be carried to the press for printing.

This process of setting pages in type, locking them into a forme, printing, stripping, and locking up new formes for printing continues until all the pages are printed. If the forme being printed is on the reverse side of an already printed sheet, those sheets are removed from where they had been waiting and are placed on the tympan so that they can be completed. Using the point holes from the first forme's printing, the paper is lined up so that the register for the second forme is correct—it's necessary for the pages on both sides of the sheet to align when the book is folded for binding, otherwise some text will be trimmed off in the margins or will be lost in the gutter where the pages are sewn into the binding.

If both sides of the sheet have been completed (also known as the sheet being perfected), then the sheets of paper are hung to dry on racks suspended from the ceiling, either in the pressroom or in composing room, or in a specially set up drying room. (The paper needs to dry since it has been dampened in order to better take the inked impressions of type.) Using a long wooden tool called a peel (much like the peel used to take bread and pizza out of hot ovens), the warehouseman takes a couple of sheets at a time and hangs them up over the drying rods. Once they've finished drying—something that could last from a day to a week, depending on the weather and the amount of paper—the sheets are removed and stacked in heaps until all the sheets in the book are completed.

Once the entire book has been printed, the dry sheets are laid out in heaps in order of their signatures, with the first page of that signature facing upward so that it can be identified. The gatherer walks along the heaps starting with the last signature in the series and working toward the first, taking a sheet from each heap and placing it on top the ones he is already holding. At the end of the process, the gatherer has assembled all the sheets that make up the book in the order of their sequence.

Once the full book in sheets has been assembled, the gatherer squares up the sheets, adds any inserts (e.g. plates of illustrations), lays down the stack, and then starts to assemble a new one. This process continues until the last complete set of sheets has been assembled. In theory, the heaps of sheets will run out at the same time. In practice, there will be more sheets of some signatures than of others. Extra sheets that aren't incorporated into the book would be later used as scrap or sold as waste paper (binders often used printed waste as part of their bindings).

With all the loose sheets gathered, each set is checked to make sure it is complete and in order, and then it is folded in half for storage (usually along the long side of the sheet so that the folds don't cut across the pages). If the book is too long to be folded as a single unit, it is divided into quires of 12 or 24 sheets and then folded. The folded sheets are then pressed and tied up, ready for storage by the publisher (or whoever is acting as the wholesale distributor) or delivery to retail booksellers.

At this point, there are lots of options for what happens in turning the gathered sheets into a book that can be read.

Once the book had been delivered to the bookseller, he could choose to have a few of them bound in a standard, plain binding. Given how much simpler it was to ship and store books in sheets or quires, rather than in heavier and less-flexible bindings, a seller was unlikely to keep a large quantity of already bound copies on hand. On the other hand, given the likelihood that some customers might prefer the convenience of having the book already bound (especially larger books), it seems likely that a seller provided that option. If that was the case, the seller would send off a few copies to the bindery to be folded properly and sewn into a binding (see "Binding" in Part 2 for details on how books were bound).

Not all customers would want books already bound. Some of them might be content with a book that was only sewn together in a rudimentary fashion, preferring to avoid the cost of a binding or wishing to have the book bound according to their own preferences. Such books might be sold stab-stitched, with thread passed through near the edge of the spine a few times to gather the quires together.

Some books—such as pamphlets, plays, single poems, or sermons—were typically never bound by the seller. In these cases, the works were sold stitched or, from the mid-1600s, in paper wrappers. As with other unbound books, the purchaser might choose to leave them stab-stitched, to have them bound immediately according to her preference, or (particularly with smaller works) to have a group of them bound together as a single volume (known as a sammelband). Other books were typically sold already bound, including bibles, devotional works, law books, and school books. In these cases, a bookseller is likely to have had a few bound at a time so that he had copies on hand ready to sell, but not so many that extra capital was tied up in unsold bound books.

The Economics of Printing

The most salient fact of hand-press printing is that the first book couldn't be sold until the last book had been printed. Although books were made of individual sheets of paper, those sheets of paper weren't printed sequentially as individual books, but as a series of formes. In other words, while it might take eight sheets of paper to make up one playbook, for an edition of 1,000 books each side of a sheet would have to be printed 1,000 times before the next side could be printed. Half-way through production you wouldn't have 500 books. You'd have 1,000 copies of half of a book. The economic consequence of this was that whoever put up the money for a book—covering the costs of labor and materials—couldn't begin to earn back her investment until well after her money was spent. Early sales of a book couldn't be used to subsidize its later production; it was all or nothing.

What did this mean for the production of books? It meant that costs needed to be controlled. As a general rule, efficiency is prized—it's why skeletons weren't stripped, it's why paper wasn't wasted—and investing in replacing old fonts and other materials is limited. It starts to make sense that over time the roles of printers and publishers began to split; a printer might prefer someone else to bear the risk of whether a book might sell when his costs are already sunk into his shop. It also meant that the size of a print run was determined by a calculation balancing the costs of labor and material. A small print run meant large unit costs. But a large print run meant that a greater percentage of the publisher's investment was tied up in stock that was going to take a longer time to produce and sell. While small print runs of 200–300 copies were typical of the early decades of printing, by the 16th century and through the late 18th century a typical print run for most categories of books was 1,000–1,500 copies.

Even if a printer weren't speculating on the success of a book's sales, the economic risks of printing large books were a concern. Obviously the more sheets there are to print, the longer it will take to finish the job. And the longer it takes to finish, the longer before you get paid. One solution is to stagger your workflow so that you are always nearing the end of a job. The practice of concurrent printing—printing different works at the same time—is a way of managing the flow of income and expenses. Printing quick things like ordinances, playbills, indulgences, and forms was another way of creating a steady income stream, if you could get such job work.

Publishers could limit their risks by acquiring titles for which there was a guaranteed market. Bibles, law books, almanacs, and school books had substantial numbers of ready buyers; the value of those titles meant that they were often regulated by a system of privileges that gave the rights to print them to specific publishers. If you couldn't guarantee a market for a book, however, you could try to create one, including by using title pages as advertisements. (See "Privileges" and "Title Pages" in Part 3 for more on these practices.)

Other strategies for balancing income and expense included the development in the mid-17th century of private subscriptions: a publisher would recruit buyers in advance, with the income from their subscription helping to cover the initial expenses of printing a book. Such subscribers were sometimes listed in the published book, as in Jacob Tonson's 1688 edition of Milton's *Paradise Lost* (Wing M2146) which at the end of the book lists "The Names of the Nobility and Gentry That Encourag'd, by Subscription, The Printing this Edition of Milton's Paradise Lost" (sig. 2Z2r).

Publishing in parts was another 17th-century response to distributing the costs of printing over its manufacture. If you can't sell the first copy of a book until the entire run has been completed, you can shorten that length of time by printing and selling the book in sections. Moxon's *Mechanick Exercises* was the first serially printed book in England, published in 38 monthly parts from 1678–1683. The individual parts of such books could be priced low enough—Moxon's was 6d per part—that it made otherwise expensive books seem affordable.

In some places, the development of guilds and other regulatory structures helped maximize opportunities. In London, the guild for printers—the Stationers' Company—was primarily focused on helping publishers recoup their costs. By limiting the number of presses that could operate, controlling who had the rights to publish a book, and distributing monopolies over popular genres of books, the Company strove to shape the market for books. (James Raven's work on the economics of bookselling in early modern England illuminates these and other complex dynamics.) In the 18th century, congers became a way for both printers and publishers to try to minimize their economic risks. Informal groups of printers or publishers/booksellers that worked in coordination, congers helped distribute the risk of such work over a group and made it possible to enforce pricing standards for the books they controlled.

If you're going to keep one thing in mind from this overview, let it be this: When you're looking at a printed text, what you're seeing is a series of decisions driven to both small and large degrees by production demands and economic pressures.

Part 2
Step-by-Step

In this part of the book, detailed information is provided about some of the central aspects of hand-press printing. It can be read straight through, or in conjunction with Part 1. The topics are presented roughly in the order in which you would encounter them in the book-making process, proceeding from making paper to bindings. It does not cover all steps of making a book, however, and it is a supplement to, not a replacement for, what is covered in Part 1.

Paper

A note on the history of paper

Although papermaking in Europe wasn't introduced until 1200 CE, and didn't become established until around 1350, paper was used for writing in Asia from around the time of Christ, moving outward from China to Japan and the Arab peninsula, reaching the Arab Mediterranean around 800 CE and displacing papyrus's dominance by 1000.

The development of paper was an important step that enabled the success of the printing press. Before the process of turning rags into paper emerged in Europe in the late 13th century, writing was done on parchment or vellum, made from animal skins. While that material worked well for centuries of handwritten texts, it was not ideally suited for the press. Parchment could be printed on, and some early books were made this way—the Gutenberg Bible was printed in both paper and parchment versions. But it took a lot of animals to provide enough parchment for an edition, and paper was a more economical choice.

The primary locations of paper mills in the hand-press period were in France, Holland, and Italy. While there were mills in England starting in the later 16th century, those early mills did not produce printing- or writing-quality paper, in part because the English wore wool clothes more than linen, and so did not have a ready source of

Studying Early Printed Books 1450–1800: A Practical Guide, First Edition. Sarah Werner.
© 2019 Sarah Werner. Published 2019 by John Wiley & Sons Ltd.

appropriate rags. English printers initially imported their paper primarily from France, particularly Normandy; in the late 17th century, the main source of paper switched to Holland. As the English paper industry developed, a tariff was imposed on foreign imports, and by the end of the 18th century, paper in England was supplied almost exclusively by English mills. The earliest mill in North America was established by a Dutch immigrant, William Rittenhouse, in Pennsylvania in 1690, and the industry spread from there.

Making Paper

The essential ingredients for making early modern paper are hemp and flax rags, water, and gelatin. In the right hands, with the right tools, and in the right combination, the resulting paper could be anywhere along the continuum of fine white writing paper to rough wrapping paper.

Paper begins with piles of rags made from hemp and/or flax. Those rags are carefully sorted according to the fineness of the material—rougher fabrics lead to rougher paper—and color. Once sorted, the rags go through a fermenting, or retting, process. The rags are mixed with water, sometimes with lime added, and turned occasionally as they ferment. This softens the cloth and begins to separate out impurities.

After retting, the rags are cut into small pieces and beaten, either with wooden stamps or, starting in the late 18th century, with a metal-bladed machine called a Hollander beater. In both, the process has the same purpose: to separate the woven cloth into clean fibers. As the rags are stamped or beaten, they are continually mixed with clean water, washing the impurities out and resulting, finally, in the liquid stuff (the technical term for this mixture) that can be turned into paper.

Once this pulp is ready, it is poured into a vat and warmed for the process of making sheets. This vat is tended by the vatman, who makes sure that the consistency of the stuff is right and forms the sheets of paper. His tools are a pair of wooden frames of woven wires (moulds) and a frame to hold it firm (a deckle); with the deckle around the mould, he dips into the vat of stuff. Lifting the mould out, the vatman gives it a side-to-side shake and a front-to-back shake to ensure that the fibers of the pulp are locked together as the water drains out through the sieve-like mould.

The physical characteristics of moulds and deckles are important because they shape the physical characteristics of the paper

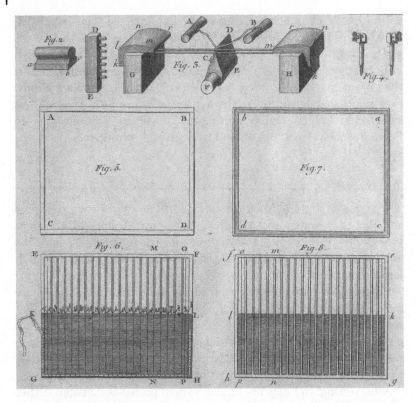

Figure 11 A mould and deckle from the *Encyclopédie*. The rectangle on the upper left is where the wire mould, once sewn, would be attached; the rectangle on the upper right is the deckle. Below are views of the mould being sewn, looking at its top surface on the left and the lower surface (where it is attached to the wooden ribs) on the right. At the top of the image is a close-up of how the wirelines would be attached to the ribs. From a public domain image made available by Smithsonian Libraries (AE25.E53X 1751 Plates, t.5, "Papeterie," plate 9).

they produce, and those can help us learn about the books we are studying. The mould is essentially a rectangle of horizontal brass wires approximately a millimeter apart that are held stable by being attached to a wooden frame around it and sewn onto vertical wooden ribs underneath it. Around this goes the deckle, a wooden frame with raised edges that transforms the mould into a shallow tray and keeps the stuff in place.

Paper made in this fashion (known as "laid paper") shows the textures and marks of that process: the side of the paper that rests on the wires keeps the slight indentation of each wire that it was resting on; the paper is also thinner in that spot and so lets more light through. These wire lines (or laid wires) are often still visible today, if you know how to look for them.

The paper also bears the impression of chain lines—the wire running along the wooden ribs that secures the laid wires. Chain lines look like heavier lines running perpendicular to the wire lines and spaced further apart—usually between 18 and 35 millimeters. Like wire lines, chain lines are usually visible without much difficulty; identifying the direction of the chain lines is part of the process of identifying a book's format (see "Format" later in this part). Because the ribs supporting the wires create some suction during the paper-making process, keeping a thicker layer of stuff adjacent to them, there is a slight shadow of darker paper along the chain lines in laid paper, although that shadow is less visible when obscured by heavy print.

In many cases, laid paper also bears the impression of various symbols of watermarks and countermarks. From the early days of European papermaking, mills would sew wire figures of pictures or letters onto the mould as a way of identifying the mill or district where the paper was made. During the 16th and 17th centuries, watermarks began to more systematically identify paper size and quality, and by the 18th century, such categorizing marks had replaced trade marks. Corresponding to that shift in the 16th and 17th centuries was a rise in countermarks, which identified the mill. While French paper continued to use countermarks as trade marks, in Dutch and English paper, countermarks gradually became a part of how the watermarks identified size and quality. Some paper,

The difference between laid and wove paper

Laid paper was predominant during the hand-press period, but began to be replaced by "wove paper" during the end of the 18th century. Wove paper was made from moulds of finely woven wires, rather than horizontal wires supported by vertical ribs. The resulting paper has no chain lines or wire lines and is easily identifiable as being made after the hand-press period. Trickier to identify is "modern laid paper" which was developed around the same time. Like the laid paper described in this section (sometimes referred to as "antique laid paper"), such paper was made from moulds using chain lines. But a different process eliminated the shadows along chain lines that you see in earlier paper. Placed side by side, it is easy to distinguish the difference between antique and modern laid paper, but to the inexperienced eye, modern laid paper can sometimes be mistaken for older paper.

especially poorer quality printing paper, did not use watermarks or countermarks at all.

Watermarks are placed in the middle of the right-hand side of the sheet, so that if the sheet of paper were folded in half along the long side to make two leaves (as in a folio format), the watermark appears in the middle of the top leaf. Countermarks are placed on the opposite side, so that in paper folded this way, they would appear in the middle of the second leaf. Depending on the format, watermarks and countermarks might be cut off at the edge of a leaf or swallowed in the gutter. The location of watermarks in a book, along with the direction of chain lines, is a primary tool for identifying format.

Just as the mould's wires leave traces of their presence on the resulting paper, so does the deckle. The deckle is designed to create a tray with walls that keeps the stuff on the mould as the water drains off. But because the frame is held on top of the mould, stuff can run underneath it, leaving the sheet with feathery edges from unevenly distributed stuff. Recognizing deckle edges is another tool for identifying the format of a book: only the edges of the sheet of paper will have deckle edges. Often the binding process removes all the deckle edges from a book, but in unbound books, and sometimes in unevenly trimmed books, the remaining deckle edges can help reveal where the leaf was relative to the sheet as a whole.

After the stuff has been shaken, the water has drained off, and the paper fibers have locked together, the vatman removes the mould from the deckle, passes the mould with the paper to the coucher, and then fits the second mould into his deckle to repeat the process. (In order to allow the vatman to keep working while the coucher turns out the paper from the mould, each deckle is paired with two moulds.) The coucher, meanwhile, turns the paper out from the mould he's holding onto a piece of felt and passes it to the layer. The layer takes the felt and paper and adds it to the stack of completed sheets. When there is enough paper ready, all three workers put the stack of paper (known as a post) into a press to squeeze out the water. (The amount of paper in such a post depends on the size of the sheets and their thickness.)

How big was a sheet of paper?

Paper came in different sizes, and sizes changed over the course of the hand-press period. Most 16th-century printing paper was a size known as foolscap and was approximately 17×13 inches. By the 18th century, the typical paper was demy, around 22×17 inches. There were also smaller and larger sheets used in printing, with larger sheets being used for special large-paper books.

After the water is squeezed out, the post is often shuffled so sheets that were in the middle move to the top or bottom of the pile, and the post is pressed again. Once the paper is sufficiently dry, it is easily handled and the layer separates the paper from the felt into a pack that is ready to be dried. According to Timothy Barrett, a smoothly coordinated team of three workers could produce between 1,500 and 4,000 sheets of paper a day; other researchers, however, think daily output was lower, especially for higher quality paper.

Once the pressed paper has been separated from the felts into a pack, a new set of workers takes the paper to dry. Groups of four to eight sheets of paper ("spurs") are hung over ropes to dry; hanging the paper in spurs, rather than as individual sheets, helps keep the paper from curling as it dried. After the spurs dry, they are taken down, separated into individual sheets of paper, and stacked. Paper at this stage is known as "waterleaf" and is highly absorbent—good for blotting paper, but not good for writing or printing.

The next step in the process typically is sizing the paper, which both strengthened it and made it more impermeable. You might imagine that paper needs to absorb ink, but if you've ever dropped ink on a paper towel, you know that absorbency causes ink to spread, making it difficult to read. An impermeable surface keeps the ink in place, so that the letters don't blot.

Sizing in the hand-press period is made from animal gelatin: hooves, horns, and skin were boiled in a vat, and the resulting liquid clarified, skimmed, diluted, and, usually, mixed with some alum to prevent spoilage. Sheets of paper are dipped in groups into the warmed sizing vat, pressed to squeeze out the excess liquid, and hung to dry. Once dried, the sheets are pressed again to flatten them.

It's at this point that paper for printing and paper for writing are differentiated. If the paper is intended for writing, it is polished to make a smooth, flat surface for the ink. Printing paper has no need of being polished, however, since the great

A note about paper quality

One of the surprising things about handling 15th-century books is how lovely the paper is, thick and white. Well-made paper in the 16th and 17th centuries can also be lovely, although the general quality of hand-made paper was at its peak in the 15th century. Paper in later periods ranged in quality, with lower quality paper being made from a lower quality rags, leading to a poorer color and variations in thickness across a single sheet. Even the poorest quality paper, however, holds up better than many more recent papers, especially those made in the early and mid-20th century, when wood pulp was often treated with acids that quickly made it turn brittle.

pressure used to force the type into the paper and print evenly means that a smooth surface isn't necessary for printing.

Once the paper is finished, it is sorted to eliminate imperfect sheets (sheets with foreign matter in them, tears, or other imperfections) and folded in half in quires (or groups) of 24 or 25 sheets. The quires are then bundled and tied up into reams. A ream is made up of 20 quires, but the outer quires, which are most likely to be damaged by the cords, are typically made up of less perfect sheets, some of which would be too imperfect for use in printing. (Such sheets were often used in other ways, including as binding material, wrappers, and proof sheets.) So a ream of paper might have only 432 sheets suitable for printing, rather than a full 480 sheets.

Cost of Paper

One of the details you hear repeatedly about printing books in this period is that the cost of paper is around half the total cost of making the book. This sometimes leads people to assume that paper was very expensive. The part of the equation we should focus on, however, is not the cost of the individual sheet, but the number of sheets that have to be bought.

A note about buying paper

A publisher often bore the costs of providing the paper, buying and supplying the paper after the printer calculated the number of sheets needed for the print run. The number of sheets would also include some extras to allow for proofing and mistakes. So while a 1,000 print run of an eight-sheet book might need a minimum of 6,400 sheets, the amount of paper bought could be closer to 7,000 sheets.

A single playbook—a fairly slim quarto—averages around eight sheets of paper. If the print run of that book was 1,000 copies (a reasonably sized print run, perhaps a bit large for plays, if not other genres), then it would take, at a minimum, 6,400 sheets of paper to print the book, or almost 15 reams. The bigger the book, or the print run, the more reams would be needed. Shakespeare's First Folio (the 1623 collection of his plays; STC 22273) used 227 sheets—or almost half of a ream of paper—per copy.

The sheer volume of paper needed made it the most expensive component of printing a book; individual sheets of paper weren't costly, but in bulk, the paper for a book rapidly added up. Particularly because the cost of the paper needed to be borne at the beginning of the process (you couldn't start printing if you didn't have paper on hand) but the investment couldn't be recouped until the end of the process (you couldn't sell the first book until the last sheet had been printed), the expense of paper was a significant part of publishing a book.

Why does it Matter?

So, how is knowing how paper is made useful? Understanding how paper was made in this period can help you identify leaves that have been added to a book after it was printed. For instance, if a leaf made from wove paper appears in a book printed in 1550, that leaf obviously must have been added by a later owner. (There are lots of reasons that might have happened; Part 5, "The Afterlives of Books," discusses this further.) For beginning bibliographers, being able to distinguish between early modern or original leaves and facsimile or forged ones is probably the most useful skill to come out of a familiarity with paper.

Another way in which paper can be used is to date when books were printed. One aspect of the paper trade to note is that since printing often required such large amounts of paper at one time, and since it was an expense that a publisher could only recoup after the entire print run of a book was completed, paper for a book was typically bought in bulk when it was needed, rather than being kept in storage. We should also remember that the physical process of making paper was hard on the moulds and watermarks: a mould in regular use would last around 12 to 18 months before it wore out. Given these two facts, we can assume that paper from the same moulds would appear in books printed around the same time. A book will usually be made up of runs of paper from the same mill and mould, although random leaves left over from other jobs might appear as well. If one book with an identified paper is known to have been printed in 1624, a different book with the same paper can also be assumed to have been printed in 1624—a useful tool for dating books that do not include a date in their imprint, or that are falsely dated.

How might you identify papers as belonging to the same mould? One methodology relies on comparing watermarks, although watermark identification can be a difficult skill. There are standard watermark shapes—grapes, pots, fleurs-de-lis—that can be mistaken for each other to novice eyes. And individual watermarks often change shape over the course of their lives, thanks to the pressures of use, making the same marks look like different ones. With training, of course, the study of watermarks (or filigranology) can be powerful: Allan Stevenson demonstrated that the Constance Missal, once thought to have been printed by Gutenberg, perhaps before his bible, was instead printed in the 1470s.

Another way to identify paper is to rely on chain lines and wire lines. While chain lines are approximately evenly spaced, in order to fully support the wire lines, they are never exactly evenly spaced. On an individual mould, the space between the chain wires might vary from 27 to 30 mm. Every sheet of paper that a mould makes will have a unique pattern of the spaces between the chain lines. And unlike watermarks, which can get damaged or wander, the spacing of the wire ribs and chain wires remains steady. In this way, David Vander Meulen was able to identify the papers used in several editions of Alexander Pope's *The Dunciad*.

Type

We are so used to thinking of type as marks on a piece of paper or screen, that we forget that it is, in Harry Carter's words, "something that you can pick up and hold in your hand."

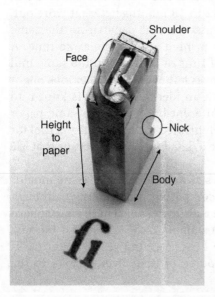

Figure 12 A piece of type for the ligature "fi" labeled to show its parts. Labels added by author to a photograph made available by Daniel Ullrich under a CC BY-SA 3.0 license.

Making Type

The first step in making type is designing the letters and symbols it will be used to print. You can read more about typefaces—the different designs for type—later in this section. Here we are going to focus on the physical process of making type, moving through a series of steps: a metal stamp is carved to create a mold into which hot metal will be poured repeatedly to form a set of individual pieces of type. It's a process that, like other aspects of making books, strives toward reproducibility.

In order to turn a design for a letter into a piece of type that can print it, the punchcutter needs to remove the empty spaces inside

A vocabulary note

In this section we will explore how the pieces of metal you can hold in your hand are made and how the marks they make appear on the page. But first it will be helpful to familiarize yourself with the vocabulary. A piece of type is what you hold in your hand. A sort is a collection of the same kind of pieces of type (all the "a"s or "1"s or "*"s in a font, for example), but an individual sort is another way of saying a piece of type. A font is the collection of letters and numbers and figures that are designed to work together; they are the same size and the same typeface. A typeface is the style of the type (what we often today call font): today's New Times Roman or Helvetica are typefaces. A typeface can consist of subsets of fonts of that face in different sizes, but it's not the same thing as a font.

and surrounding the letter, leaving only the lines to be printed in relief. By using sharp files and tools to punch out the interior spaces of the letter (the counter), he carefully carves away the metal from the end of a steel stick to reveal the letter in relief. (The letter, of course, is its mirror image: for the type to print correctly, the letter itself must be in reverse on the type.)

After it's been cut, the punchcutter checks the letter by taking a smoke proof from it, heating the end in the flame of a candle or lamp so that the soot adheres to its surface and, when pressed carefully on a piece of paper, prints the resulting letter. But while the punch might print a perfect letter, it is not used as a piece of type; it would be time-consuming and therefore prohibitively expensive to produce enough type to print a book by carving each individual letter. The solution is to create a mold from which copies of the type can be made.

After the steel punch has been cut, it is stamped into a piece of copper to make the matrix, an indented space that will be filled with hot metal to form the letter. The resulting strike, as it is called, then needs to be standardized. The imprint of the letter needs to be the same distance from the edges of the piece of type so that all sorts made for a font sit evenly when printed—if they are not carefully aligned, the printed text can appear to dance up and down, instead of being lined up evenly across the page.

A note about molds

It's possible that in the earliest years of printing, Gutenberg cast type not from metal molds, but from temporary ones. After using punches to press a shape into hardened sand, a typecaster would pour in the hot metal to form the letter. Such molds were destroyed in the process of casting each piece of type, and metal molds would have been an obvious improvement. Blaise Agüera y Arcas, working with Paul Needham, used type analysis to come up with this hypothesis, but Christoph Reske has pointed out some methodological flaws and argues against it.

Once the strike has been made, it can be used as a matrix for making as many pieces of type as needed. A type mold consists of the copper strike placed inside a metal and wood holder that can be adjusted to create matrices of different sizes. (Not only do letters differ in width, fonts differ in size, and the mold needs to adjust to work with all of them.)

In addition to holding the matrix in place, the mold also creates a nick—an indentation on the side of the type near its foot that indicates which way to orient the face. The nick is important for the compositor, who needs to be sure that he is placing the type so that it prints the right way up. By feeling for the nick, the compositor can set his type faster than if he had to examine the face of each piece of type he picks up.

Once the mold is assembled, a mixture of lead, tin, and antimony is heated and melted, and then poured in and driven into the corners of the matrix with a sharp swing or jerk from the typecaster. The mold is then opened, the solid type removed, and the process repeated for as long as needed.

While the letters are finished at this point, the rest of the piece of the type needs to be made uniform. The excess pieces of metal from the casting (the jets) are broken off, and the body and feet are filed smooth so that they move easily and fit precisely with each other.

While most sorts are of individual characters—an "a" or a "2"—there are some combinations of characters that are printed from a single sort. The most common ones are "ſ" (the long-s) or "f" in combination with a letter with a tall ascender, such as an "h." If you look carefully at the "f" and the "i" depicted in Figure 12, you can see that if the two pieces of type were placed next to each other, there would be too much white space between the letters (they wouldn't be kerned properly). If you could adjust the letters so that the excess white space disappeared, the tops of the "f" and the dot of the "i" would overlap, something that isn't possible with two rectangular pieces of metal. A ligature ties the two letters together, so that the top of the "f" merges into the dot of the "i," resulting in a single sort of two letters. You can easily recognize a ligature from the lines that join them together—if two or more letters touch each other, they are printed from a single piece of type.

There are not only different sorts to be cast, but different sizes of type. The title of a book or a chapter heading is often larger than the body text, which is itself usually larger than notes printed in the margins. Type size refers to the height of the body—approximately how tall a letter is from the top of the ascender to the bottom of the descender. There were different sizes of type available throughout the period, although the exact measurements varied from location to location and over time. (There is a useful table with this information in Gaskell's *New Introduction*.)

The skill of typemaking—the creation of punches and matrices—was distinct from that of printing and one already mastered by goldsmiths and other metalworkers. In the early years of printing, punches and strikes might have been made by metalworkers who then sold them to printers for casting. By the middle of the 16th century, printers would buy fonts from foundries, rather than buying strikes or matrices and doing their own casting. The biggest foundries were in France and Holland, and typemakers often used specimen sheets to show printed examples of the range of fonts available to buy. As with other aspects of the hand-press book trade, the process shifted from a general skill to a specialized trade consolidated in a few dominant businesses.

Typefaces

In the early centuries of movable type, typefaces were based on book hands—the letter shapes that scribes used in writing. There is sometimes a tendency for people to describe the earliest books and their type as striving to look like manuscripts of the period, as if Gutenberg and his contemporaries were trying to imitate manuscripts. But a better way of understanding the design of incunabula (books printed before 1501), including the type that they used, is that they strove to look like familiar books. If big lectern bibles were written in a gothic textura, big lectern bibles would be printed in textura because that was the expectation for what such books looked like. The reliance of printed type on book hands was not because printers wanted to fool people into thinking that printed works were handwritten ones, but because printed books needed to be easy to read and the shapes of words and letters that readers were used to were those written in the hands that were already in circulation.

As print spread from its beginnings in Germany, different typefaces emerged according to regional practices. In Italy, the dominance of humanistic scribes led to the development of roman and italic faces for printed books. Eventually, most areas printed works in gothic or roman according to what type of text it was, sometimes using both typefaces in a single work. With the increased popularity of print, designers began creating typefaces specifically for the press, with a focus more on the ease of printing rather than the ease of writing with a quill, and printed texts were usually immediately obviously distinct from manuscript ones.

Identifying individual typefaces is a difficult skill; there are many different roman typefaces, with often minute differences. For a beginning bibliographer, it is useful simply to be able to recognize the different families of typefaces and to understand what information they might signal.

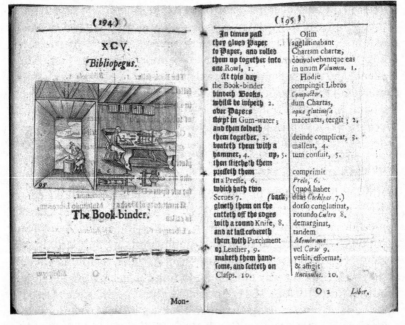

Figure 13 An example of different typefaces used in the account of a book binder in Comenius's 1685 *Orbis sensualium pictus* (Wing C5525). The column of Latin text on the right uses a roman typeface for the base text and an italic for the vocabulary words labeled in the illustration; the column of English text uses a gothic typeface with a roman face for the contrasting words. The type border below the illustration shows the accidental inking and printing of the shoulder of the pieces of type. Image made available by the Folger Shakespeare Library under a CC BY-SA 4.0 license (Wing C5525; sigs. O1v-O2r).

Gothic (or black letter) typefaces are rarely used today, and so perhaps are most easily recognized—and most difficult to read—because they are unfamiliar. In today's English-speaking world, we see black letter used mostly on the masthead of newspapers (the *New York Times* uses a black letter for its title), on formal diplomas, and in the logos of death metal bands. In the hand-press period, black letter was used frequently on its own or in combination with other faces, and it is necessary to recognize it and be comfortable reading it.

Black letter is an apt name for this typeface because it produces letters with more black spaces than other fonts do. Black letter tends to have thick vertical lines, fewer rounded curves, and to be upright rather than sloped. Especially in early black letter faces, but also in later ones, there are multiple forms of the same letter; early black letter also used a lot of abbreviations. (See "Alphabet" in Part 3 for an image of typical black letter and more information on abbreviations.)

In many countries, gothic dominated the first century of printing, but then gradually was replaced by roman typefaces. Italy used very little black letter even from the beginning (and when it did, it used a rotunda typeface rather than the more angular textura or bastarda). Britain used black letter up until the 1550s and thereafter primarily in certain categories of texts, including Bibles, legal texts, and proclamations. In the Netherlands and Belgium, a similar pattern emerged by the 1650s. In contrast, gothic was the only font used throughout the hand-press period in Germany, German-speaking Switzerland, and Scandinavia.

Roman typeface is what we are primarily used to reading today. (This book is in a roman typeface.) Like gothic, it's a typeface that emerged from the hands used by scribes in the 1400s—in this case, by humanistic scribes in Italy. A more open face than gothic, with less variability for individual letters, roman typefaces became the dominant form for printing in many places.

A cursive form of roman fonts, known as italic, emerged in the early 1500s. An open, rounded face, like roman, but with a greater slant and more ligatures, italic typefaces were initially used as the main face in setting texts. But the difficult legibility of the face meant that it soon turned into a complement to roman typefaces, used to set off words but not as the primary typeface.

Other typefaces were created for what are often referred to as "exotic" alphabets. Few printers were printing texts entirely in Greek, but many were printing texts that included Greek words or phrases.

How do you choose a typeface?

Typefaces for a work were typically chosen according to what different regions and different genres had established as usual. If proclamations were in black face, then that was that; if all works were generally in roman, then that's what you would use. But sometimes a different face was chosen for its associations. Zachary Lesser argues that black letter continued to be used in England even after the general switch to roman faces as a way of creating a typographical nostalgia.

The early Greek typeface that came to dominate the hand-press period was based on a cursive style, with an abundance of ligatures, alternate letter forms, and contractions. It might have been attractive to look at, but it was difficult to make and to print with— a complete font of Greek could have up to three times as many sorts of type as a Latin font. Different Greek typefaces gradually reduced the number of ligatures and alternates, and in the 1750s, a new face eliminated contractions and all but a few ligatures.

Other languages were less frequently printed and remained specialized. The first books to use Hebrew letters were printed in Italy in the 1470s, and while the Jewish community soon developed its own typography that continues to influence printed Hebrew, there were also steps taken in places like Venice to restrict the printing of Hebrew to Christian printers. As with other alphabets, two different typefaces were available to differentiate between text and commentary or between Hebrew and Yiddish.

Fonts

A printer did not buy individual sorts of type but a font—a set of letters, numbers, symbols, and other sorts of the same body size and design, in combinations according to the frequency of their use.

A typical font using the Latin alphabet (the alphabet we use to write English and most Western European languages) might have around 150 sorts, including capital letters, small capitals, lower case letters, accented letters, ligatures, numbers, punctuation, and some common symbols (such as "&" and "*"). A font would also include differently sized spaces to go between words and spaces to fill out a blank line (quads).

When a printer bought a font of type, he expected the sorts to be distributed in proportion to the frequency with which they were used. In English, for example, the letters "a" and "e" are used much more often than "x" and "z." If a font included the same number of pieces for each letter, a printer would run out of "a"s and "e"s long before any of the other letters. To prevent this imbalance, fonts were sold proportionally. In his 1755 *Printer's Grammar*, John Smith describes a "bill of letter" as including 12,000 "e"s, 7,000 "a"s, 3,000 "m"s, and 400 "x"s. Different languages, of course, would have different frequencies of letter usage, and so differently distributed fonts.

Depending on the time period, printers would order fonts by the letter (with the sort "m" typically specified and the rest being made out proportionally) or by weight. A full order could easily weigh a few hundred pounds and take up over a dozen cases. And it was expensive: if you were setting up a new print shop, two-thirds of the initial costs would be for buying type. But printers could also stretch the lifetime of their type over decades. Because of the expense of investing in a new font, printers often resisted switching over to a new typeface until their current type was too worn to be practical.

Printers kept the type being used in wooden cases divided into small boxes, often of varying sizes, in which the sorts were distributed according to a standardized pattern. One type of case was a "single lay"—a single large box that contained all the sorts, with capital letters along the top and small letters below. That style of case was gradually replaced in many regions by a "divided lay"—a pair of cases, one above the other, with the capitals and small capitals in the upper case and the small letters in the lower case.

A note about cases

This arrangement of sorts is what gives rise to our use of "upper case" and "lower case" to refer to capital and small letters. The print roots of those phrases is one of the reasons why people who study manuscripts in this period refer to those letters not with those terms, but by "majuscule" and "miniscule," which evoke handwriting rather than printing.

There were national variants in how the compartments in the lower case were distributed, affected by the local language and how frequently it used each letter. As a general rule, the letters that were used the most often were kept in large compartments near the middle of the case. The standardized arrangement and the placement of frequently used letters in easily reached boxes meant that compositors could set type by reading the text and reaching automatically for where the letters were.

Why does it Matter?

Understanding how type was made and used can help us understand how books were printed. Because individual marks on a printed page are made by individual pieces of metal, and those individual pieces of metal sometimes have identifying characteristics, it can be possible to trace when a single piece of type was used. Although sorts were intended to be uniform, time and usage sometimes damaged pieces of type, not badly enough that they had to be discarded but enough that they left marks that were distinct from others of the same sort. In his monumental study of Shakespeare's First Folio, Charlton Hinman found a number of examples of broken type that allowed him to reconstruct the order in which the pages were printed as well as to identify other books that were printed in the shop at the same time. Through this work, Hinman was able to illuminate aspects of the printing trade (include the practice of concurrent printing) that would otherwise require business records to confirm, records that rarely exist.

Fonts can also be distinguished from other fonts: pieces of type show wear, different faces are introduced accidentally or to replace broken types. Such font identification can help identify unknown printers, particularly in earlier periods: if a font is used by a named printer, other books printed with the same font are most likely to have been printed in the same shop.

Finally, understanding the physical characteristics of pieces of type and type cases can help us understand how errors can be introduced into a printed text and identify which errors need to be corrected in editing. "Thnt" is the result of a fouled case—an "n" being mixed in with the "a" sorts in the type case—and it would obviously need to be changed to "that." But is "Iudean" a form of "Judean" (with the "J" being written as "I" because it comes at the start of a word) or is it a mistake for "Indian" (with the "u" either a turned "n" or a fouled case)? (This example comes from a famous crux at the end of Shakespeare's play *Othello*, which has the eponymous hero describe himself as a base Indian who threw away a pearl in the Quarto version of the text but as a base "Iudean" in the Folio text; editors tend to prefer "Indian" but there are also arguments in favor of what we would spell "Judaean.")

The problem of library categorization

Libraries often use the terms "folio" and "quarto" to refer to the height of books rather than their formats. It's confusing for bibliographers, who use the terms differently, but if a library has a book shelved as a "quarto," that simply means that it is shorter than a set height, and is not a determination of its format.

Format

It is tempting, but incorrect, to think of format as referring to size. Format is the ratio of the number of printed leaves to the sheet of paper: if a sheet of paper is laid out to print four leaves, it's a quarto; if it makes eight leaves, it's an octavo. If both sheets of paper are the same size, the octavo will indeed be smaller than the quarto, but if one sheet of paper is larger than the other, you can have an octavo that will be the same size as, or larger than, the quarto.

Because hand-press books were printed one side of a sheet of paper at a time, understanding how the text was arranged (or imposed) on a side of a sheet of paper is the key to understanding format. When talking about imposition, we refer to formes—the arrangement of text that prints a side of a sheet of paper. Each sheet is printed from two different formes, an outer forme (which includes the first page of text and is on the outside of the sheet once folded) and the inner forme (which includes the front of the second leaf of text and is on the inside of the sheet once folded). How each forme is arranged depends on the format being printed and the imposition being used.

Imposition

Different formats require different impositions, and there are a large number of formats and impositions used in the hand-press period, too many to be detailed here. But you will encounter a handful of common formats and impositions the most frequently. (Identifying format requires a familiarity with chain lines and watermarks; it might be helpful to review "Paper" in this part for this.)

Since most of us are focused on format in terms of how we read books, rather than in terms of how we would print books, the illustrations that follow focus on helping you imagine how a printed sheet of paper would be folded into pages of text. But it's important to know that these pictures don't show what the puller would see when the sheet was on the press. For example, in England, a quarto

A note about signature marks

Books in the hand-press period only gradually developed the practice of using page numbers, but they consistently used what we call signature marks to identify the location of gatherings and leaves. Signature marks can be found at the bottom of a page and typically use a combination of letters to identify the gathering and numbers to identify the leaf. For example, the signature C2 would appear on the second leaf of the C gathering. Compositors usually only include signatures for the first half of the leaves in a gathering; once the first half of a sheet is folded, the remaining leaves fall obviously into place and don't need to be signed. Since signature marks identify an entire leaf, not a page, we use the term "recto" to refer to the front of the leaf and "verso" for the back. Most bibliographers abbreviate these to "r" and "v"—C2r—although Gaskell uses "a" and "b." In my diagrams, I have included the signature and page number for every leaf to help illustrate how the pages relate to each other, but this does not follow early printing practices. (For more on how signature marks work and what we can learn from them, see "Signature Marks" in Part 3.)

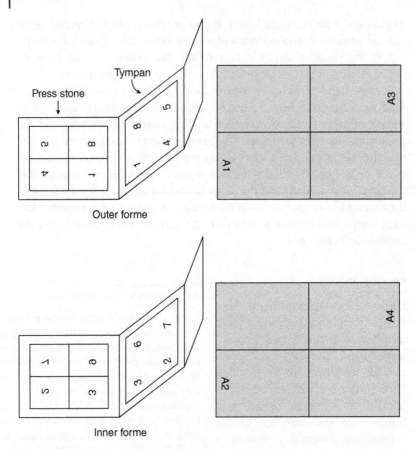

Figures 14 and 15 The view from the puller's perspective of a quarto imposition and the printed sheet on the tympan. Signatures A1 (page 1) and A2 (page 3) are placed on the press stone so that they are next to the tympan. Based on sketches by the author.

imposition would be placed on the press stone so that the first page (A1r) is on his right-hand side; when it came time to perfect the sheet, the third page (A2r) would also be placed on the stone on his right-hand side. But in France and Germany, the imposition might be inverted: the locked chase would be placed on the stone with A1r on the upper left. Either way, the end result would be the same: a quarto that starts with A1r and ends with A4v.

Rather than focus on what a pressman saw, I encourage you to visualize holding a printed sheet in your hands and folding it into a gathering. So my illustration of a quarto looks like Figure 16, with the outer forme on top and inner forme below it; if you imagine it as a

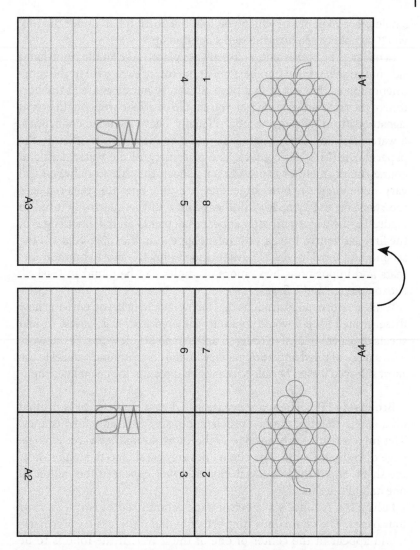

Figure 16 This diagram shows how the sheet would be aligned as if you were folding it, rather than printing it; visualize the bottom side of the sheet flipping up under the top side so that page 2 is on the back of page 1. With some practice, you can look at these diagrams and imagine how both sides of a single sheet align. Based on a sketch by the author.

single piece of paper in which you fold the bottom half under the top, you'll be able to see how the two sides line up.

In order to be consistent, I have always placed A1r on the right-hand side of the sheet. Page numbers are at the top of each page in the same orientation as the text of that page. Signature numbers are at the bottom of the recto side of each leaf; you should be able to work out the verso signatures from the page numbers. Finally, I have included chain lines, a watermark (a bunch of grapes), and a countermark to identify the papermaker ("SW" of course). The placement of the watermark and countermark (if either is present on a sheet; they are not always) will vary depending on how large they are and how the puller places the sheet on the tympan. In other words, in the quarto pictured in Figure 16, the watermark may appear as depicted on the inner edges of the first and fourth leaves, or it might appear on the inner edges of the second and third leaves. (I have included only the most common formats and impositions here; more examples can be found in Gaskell, Moxon, Fertel, and J. Smith.)

While the format illustrations that follow should help you envision how these printed sheets would fold into gathered text, it is easiest to fold sheets of paper yourself in order to understand how it works. If you work with a piece of ruled notebook paper, with the lines running parallel to the short side, you'll even be able to see which direction the chain lines run.

Broadside (1°): There are occasions when a single page is printed on a single sheet of paper—proclamations and ballads, for instance. The imposition of a broadside is the most straightforward: a single page of text per forme. The chain lines run parallel to the long side of the sheet, and if there is a watermark, it will appear in the middle of one half of the sheet.

Folio (2°): A folio is a sheet of paper comprised of two leaves, or four pages. The chain lines run vertically, and if there is a watermark, it will appear in the center of one of the leaves. If the folio is to be gathered by individual sheets, then the outer forme will consist of pages 1 and 4, and the inner of pages 2 and 3. But while that was a standard structure in the 18th century, in earlier years of printing, books in folio format often had gatherings of two to five sheets folded inside each other. English folios in the 16th and 17th centuries were usually made up of three sheets in a single gathering, with pages 1 and 12 on the outer forme of the outermost sheet, and 2 and 11 on the inner; then a sheet with 3 and 10 on the outer forme and so on. Such a format is described as a folio in sixes (2° in 6 s). (See Figures 17–18.)

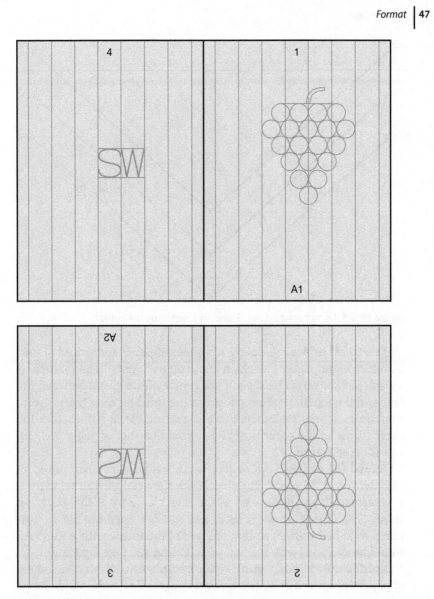

Figure 17 Folio imposition. Based on a sketch by the author.

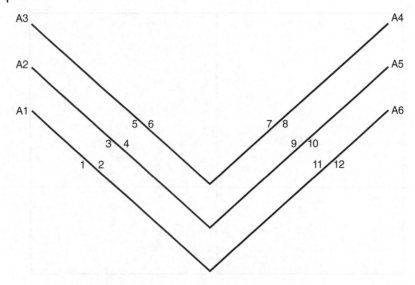

Figure 18 A folio gathered in sixes. Based on a sketch by the author.

Quarto (4° or 4to): A quarto is a sheet of paper comprised of four leaves, or eight pages. The chain lines run horizontally, and if there is a watermark it might be seen in the center of the gutter between the first and the fourth or the second and the third leaves. Quartos were sometimes quired two sheets in a gathering (4° in 8s), so that the outer forme of the outermost sheet would consist of pages 1, 4, 13, and 16. (See Figure 19.)

Octavo (8° or 8vo): An octavo is a sheet of paper comprised of eight leaves, or 16 pages. The chain lines run vertically, and if there is a watermark it might be seen in the upper corners of the gutter on leaves 1, 4, 5, and 8 or on leaves 2, 3, 6, and 7. Sometimes the imposition would be inverted, so that the half of the forme with A1 and A5 would be swapped with the half with A7 and A3. (See Figure 20.)

Duodecimo (12° or 12mo): A duodecimo, or twelvemo, is a sheet of paper comprised of 12 leaves, or 24 pages. There are a wide range of impositions used to print a 12mo, including ones which require cutting as well as folding in order to sequence the pages correctly (in Figures 21 and 22, the lines of dashes indicate where it would be cut). Regardless of the imposition, the chain lines run horizontally; the placement of watermarks varies, as shown in the diagrams.

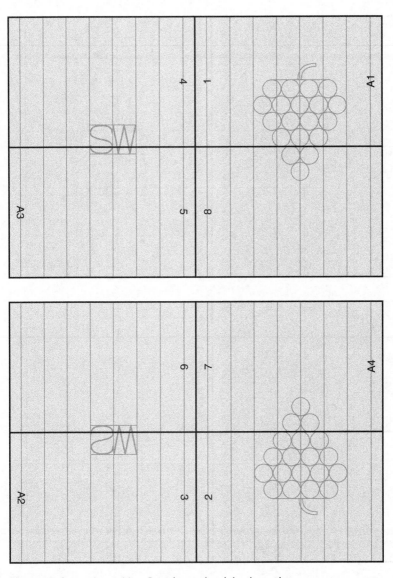

Figure 19 Quarto imposition. Based on a sketch by the author.

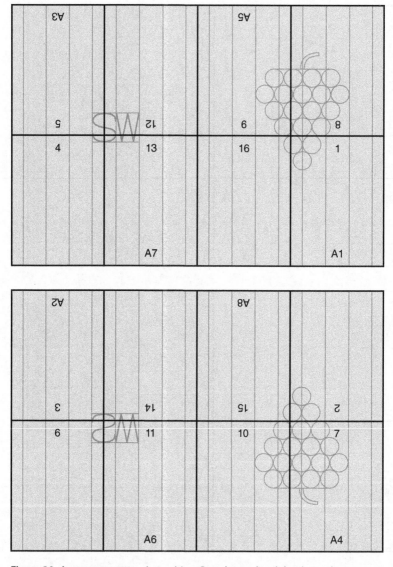

Figure 20 A common octavo imposition. Based on a sketch by the author.

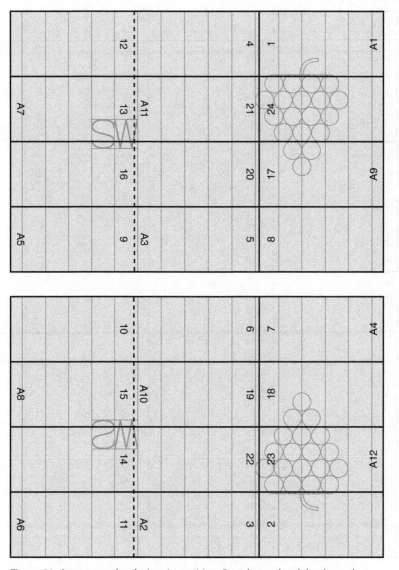

Figure 21 A common duodecimo imposition. Based on a sketch by the author.

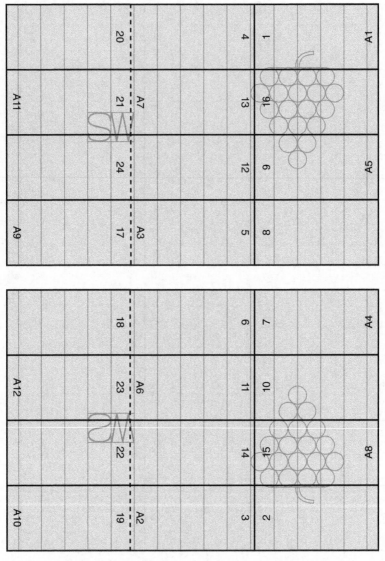

Figure 22 A duodecimo set in 8 and 4. Based on a sketch by the author.

There are also smaller formats—16°, 32°, 64°—and more uncommon impositions and formats—such as a 10°—as well as variants on the impositions described above. More information on those can be found in Gaskell and other sources listed in Appendix 1.

Once you begin to imagine a text in terms of formes, it's clear that there are two ways to proceed. You could set the text serially, imposing page 1, then page 2, then page 3, etc. Doing it this way has the advantage of knowing exactly where each page begins and ends (although if you're at the end of a section, or the end of the book, you might find yourself needing to crowd the text to get it all to fit onto the final sheet). However, it also means that you can't print the inner forme until the penultimate page of the sequence has been set, and the outer forme until the last page is set.

Another way of proceeding is to set the text by formes. For a quarto's outer forme, this would mean setting pages 1, 4, 5, and 8 and then (perhaps while the outer forme is on the press) setting the inner forme's pages 2, 3, 6, and 7. The difficulty here, of course, is that you need to know where page 4 starts before you've set the preceding pages. If you've over- or underestimated the pages on the outer forme, you'll need to make up the difference on the inner forme, either stretching out the text or crowding it together to fit onto the sheet.

Both ways of setting the text require a careful casting off of the source text, a process in which a skilled printer reads through the text to be printed and estimates where each page will start and stop, marking it on the copy text so that the compositors know where to work from.

Identifying Format

The first key to identifying what format a book is in is the direction of the chain lines: are they vertical or horizontal? That answer will initially eliminate many formats. The next step is to look for watermarks and where they are placed. As you can see from the diagrams, different impositions will result in watermarks appearing on different leaves and in different locations.

Finding paper marks

The easiest way to see chain lines, watermarks, and other paper characteristics is to use a special light that shines through the paper without damaging it. Often libraries can provide you with an electroluminescent or cold light panel. (If you ask for a light to examine watermarks, they'll know what you mean.) Just place it under the leaf you're examining (you might need to turn off your desk lamp), and the marks should be visible as lighter areas of the paper.

Don't completely ignore size

Although format is not the same thing as size, it is also true that most folios are larger than quartos and most quartos are larger than duodecimos. Size can be a starting point for your determination, but you always need to verify with chain lines and watermarks.

Watermarks will not always be visible, however. In some formats, watermarks will end up in the gutter of the book or at the edges and trimmed away. And not all paper was made with watermarks.

It can also be helpful when identifying format to consider the number of leaves in a gathering. Although the leaves aren't strictly dependent on the format—a gathering of eight leaves could be the result of an octavo or a quarto in eights, for example—it is a clue. If the gatherings are of 12 leaves, that's a sign that the format could be a 12mo, which can then be verified by chain lines and watermarks.

It's important to remember that the first and last gatherings sometimes vary from the rest of the book. The preliminaries might be only six leaves when the main text of the book is in 12-leaf gatherings.

Why does it Matter?

Being able to identify format and imposition can help you understand a range of features of a book. For instance, stop-press changes tended to happen to an entire forme—if you've stopped the press to make a change on the first page of a quarto gathering, you might also make changes to the fourth and fifth pages while you're at it. Anomalies in page layout can be understood through imposition as well—a page may be overset (crowded with extra lines on the page) or underset (fewer lines on the page) because of problems in casting off.

Knowing the structure of gatherings and sheets can reveal irregularities of added or removed leaves. Is there a sequence of six leaves in the middle of a quarto? Two of those leaves might have been inserted after the others were printed. Is there a gathering of only three leaves? That's a clue to look to see what happened to the missing leaf.

While we have considered format from a purely bibliographical perspective, different formats can also provide information about how a book was conceived and received. Different genres of book tended to all use the same format: playbooks, for instance, were usually quartos. This choice of format was often a practical one determined by the amount of text and the number of sheets of paper it would use. Scholars have argued that formats connote textual aspirations: Shakespeare's collected works are printed in folio because they are aiming to be prestigious; playbooks are in quartos because they are disposable. But work done by Steven Galbraith and Joseph Dane and Alexandra Gillespie argue that these characterizations are inaccurate and overlook the economic reasons that drive these choices. Collected works of literary authors like Shakespeare and Spenser often were cheaper to print as folios in order to accommodate the bulk of the texts, and there was nothing inherently cheap about printing quartos.

Printing

The printing press—or common press, to differentiate it from the rolling press used for engravings (see "Illustrations" later in this part)—is a fairly straightforward piece of machinery that requires a complicated set of actions to operate. The details of how the common press worked varied from region to region and across time, but the basic form and operations remained the same.

Figure 23 An illustration of a pressroom from the *Encyclopédie*. On the left, the puller is placing a blank sheet on the tympan while the beater inks the forme. On the right, another pressman is pulling the bar across the press to lower the platen onto the press stone. From a public domain image made available by Smithsonian Libraries (AE25.E53X 1751 Plates, t.7, "Imprimerie en caracteres" plate 14).

The Common Press

The press itself is essentially a wooden frame of two upright pillars of wood and cross pieces holding in place the mechanism that pushes down on the paper and the mechanism that rolls the type and paper under the press. The upright pillars (the cheeks) are around 6.5 feet high; because they need to be able to withstand a great deal of torque from the action of pulling the press, they are braced to the ceiling to keep them from shifting. From these pillars hangs the impression mechanism, a large slab of wood (the platen) around 1 × 1.5 feet. The platen moves up and down by means of a spindle and bar, which is pulled forcefully across the press to lower the platen onto the press stone and type; when the bar is released, the spindle raises the platen. This pulling action is, of course, why the pressman working in this role is referred to as the puller.

Below the platen is the printing carriage, about 2.5 feet off the ground, on which rests the press stone and which can be rolled in and out from under the platen. The press stone is a smooth slab of marble or limestone about 2 × 1.5 feet (about twice the length of the platen). On this stone rests the forme once it is ready to be printed.

Attached to this assembly, by hinges, is the tympan and, attached to that, the frisket. The tympan is a frame onto which the paper is attached with two adjustable pins (points). Hinged at the top of the tympan is the frisket, another frame which helps secure the paper and masks off those areas not being printed.

Making Ready

The first time a forme is printed, the pressmen need to make sure the press is set up for it. This process (making ready) primarily entails setting up the tympan and frisket. The tympan needs to be packed with blankets or other soft material into which the type can push. Even though the forme is generally an even surface of type, the force of the platen can cause the type to bite into and tear the paper; packing the tympan helps prevent the paper from tearing by absorbing some of that force.

If it's the first forme of a work, the points on the tympan need to be adjusted according to the size of the paper and the format of the book. For most formats, the points are placed in the margins of the middle of the sheet of paper, with the nearest point from where the puller stands placed slightly further from the paper's edge and the farther point slightly nearer. This asymmetry helps to ensure that the two sides of the sheet align when printed. For 12mos, the points cannot be placed in the middle of the length of paper, since that would put them in the middle of a printed page. Instead, they are placed two-thirds of the way up the sheet. Once the points are placed, the pressman checks that they fit into the slots on the crossbars of the chase by folding down the tympan over the forme on the press stone. Once the points are in place, they should not need to be moved for the rest of the run, although they will need to be checked that they don't hit the bars.

Next, the pressman prints a sheet and pastes it to the tympan as a guide for placing subsequent sheets on the points. The tympan sheet helps ensure that the margins and text are consistent throughout the run (if the paper is placed too high or off to one side, for instance, it won't register properly).

Finally, a frisket will need to be made for varying formes. For a standard forme with printed areas that occupy full pages, a single frisket could be used for all of them. For formes that have other layouts—more blank spaces or two-color printing—new friskets will need to be made. Either way, a piece of parchment is placed on

A note about bearing type

Since type needs to be held securely in place in order to print cleanly, even white spaces on the page need to be filled with some sort of object. There is a range of spacers (quads) that can fill out individual lines to meet this need. But larger areas of white space are often filled with bearing type—blocks of type that are not inked. If the bottom half of a page is blank, the platen might tilt into that empty space when pressing down on it, leaving the lines of text at the top of the page without the pressure necessary to print cleanly. The solution to this problem is to create an even surface all the same height so that the platen doesn't rock. Quads wouldn't provide that even surface, but blocks of uninked type would. Sometimes you can see the blind impressions left by such type; occasionally you might come across a book in which the bearing type has been accidentally inked and printed.

Printing in red and black

Some works, usually religious works and almanacs, use both black and red ink to demarcate sections of the work or to call attention to specific dates ("red-letter days"). Other works might want to use red ink as a decorative element on title pages. Printing in both black and red ink usually requires running the sheet of paper through the press twice, once for the black text to print and once for the red. The printing can be done first in red, or first in black; either way, the practice is essentially the same, but for simplicity's sake, this describes the practice in terms of printing black sections first. First a sheet is printed of the entire forme. Then the areas that are to be printed in black are cut out of the frisket frame, leaving the red areas covered so they won't print. The forme is then inked and printed as usual. After the run of black text is finished, an inverse of the frame is made, covering the black areas and leaving the red ones open. Often the red type is elevated by underlays or the sheet raised by patches placed under the paper so that the red type is slightly elevated and bites more evenly into the paper. It is important to get the paper to line up precisely so that the black and red type register, rather than overlapping with each other, but not all two-color print jobs do so successfully.

the tympan and printed. The pressman then cuts away the printed areas, leaving open spaces for the inked type to print and a mask to protect the unprinted areas of the sheet. If a frisket is for a standard layout, it might be saved for reuse; if not, it would become available for other purposes. (Some of the examples we have today of friskets have survived because they were reused in bindings.)

While the press is being prepared, the necessary sheets of paper for the run are prepared as well. Because the force of the press isn't great enough to ensure an even distribution of ink on dry, sized paper, the sheets need to be dampened overnight, softening the fibers and making it easier for the type to bite into the paper. The paper is brought from where it was stored in the warehouse the day before it is to be printed, dipped through a pan of water, unfolded, and stacked into a heap under a heavy weight.

The two-pull press

The human-powered hand-press can't generate enough pressure to print the entire side of a sheet evenly. The earliest presses in the first decades of printing didn't have movable carriages to roll the press stone under the platen, so only half of a sheet was set and placed on the stone at a time. With the development of the rolling carriage, a forme for the entire side of a sheet could be set at one time, but it still took two pulls to print it: one half would be printed, the platen lifted, and then the second half rolled further under the platen. One of the advantages of machine presses is that they can generate more pressure across larger areas, and the side of a sheet—even a large one—can be printed in one go.

Presswork

Once the press and paper are ready, the printing can begin. The printer working the press—the puller—places the first sheet of paper on the points, aligning it with the tympan sheet, and folds the frisket down over it. This, in turn, is folded down onto the forme, which is resting on the press stone; the stone is rolled under the platen. The puller reaches across the press to grab the bar and pulls it hard toward himself, lowering the platen onto the forme and pressing it into the type. The puller then releases the bar, which raises the platen.

Since the platen only covers half of the press stone, the carriage is rolled further under the platen so that the second half of the forme can be printed. Once the second half is printed, the carriage is rolled out from under the platen and the sheet is removed from the tympan and placed in a nearby heap.

While the puller is placing and removing sheets of paper, the beater is inking the type. Ink is dabbed onto the type using a pair of ink balls, wooden cups about 6 inches in diameter stuffed with wool and covered with leather. The beater holds one ball in each hand and uses a rocking motion to transfer ink onto the forme. While the puller is printing the forme, the beater works the two balls against each other, keeping the ink at a good consistency and occasionally adding more ink to the balls by dabbing the ink plate attached to the side of the press. At the end of the day, the balls are disassembled, with the leather kept soft by being soaked in urine and the wool padding teased apart to remove any lumps.

Once the entire print run of a forme has been completed, the resulting heap of paper is ready to have its other side printed, a process often known as perfecting. The process is largely the same—the new forme is checked to make sure that it is in the right position, a new frisket is provided if necessary. This time, however, the puller guides the paper onto the points using the existing holes, thus ensuring that the sheets register correctly. Perfecting a sheet could happen on the same press or on a different press, depending on the shop's workflow.

A note about inks

The ink used for printing was made primarily from linseed oil and lampblack collected from the soot of burning resins. (Red printing ink used ground vermilion.) The earliest black inks used in incunables were a rich, dark color that has remained stable for centuries. Later inks, however, did not have the same darkness, but were often a thinner black, due to the pressures of keeping costs low and producing ink in large quantities. Inks were generally made by specialists and bought as needed by printers, although some printers made their own. (Ink for writing used a different recipe; it was based on water with oak galls to provide the black color.)

Skeleton Formes

After a forme has been printed, the type is usually distributed back into cases. (Leaving type standing limited the amount of type available for printing.) But the parts of the forme that do not change from one to the next are left in place on the imposing stone. These parts—usually the headlines, any rules or borders being used for multiple sheets, and the sticks and quoins that lock the forme into the

You don't need to go it alone

Books were not necessarily entirely set by a single compositor or printed on a single press. If a shop had two presses, both could be employed to print formes for the same book at the same time. And the reverse is true as well: if two presses were printing the same book, one or both could interrupt their work on that book to print a different one. Concurrent printing was especially useful for large works, which took a long time to complete; interrupting them with shorter jobs had the benefit of bringing in relatively quick money. Using different presses to print a book was true on a larger scale as well: while most works were printed by a single printer's shop, printing could also be shared across multiple shops. Shared printing was sometimes split among members of a partnership, or as a way of increasing capacity beyond that of a single shop.

chase—are known as the skeleton forme. (You might think of the skeleton as the bones of the forme that support the other features of the text.)

Because the skeleton doesn't change over the course of a book, it doesn't make sense to reset it for each new forme. (While aspects of it might change—the headline, for instance, might change with different sections of a book, and pagination or foliation needs to be adjusted—most of it is reused.) Usually more than one skeleton is used, so that one is available for locking up the next forme to be printed while another is on the press.

Why does it Matter?

The basic operations of printing drive many of the other aspects of how books were produced and how the book trade operated. The economic imperatives of marketing printed books and protecting publisher's investments are a direct result of how books are printed; the last section of Part 1 considers some of those factors, as do the discussions about advertisements, privileges, and title pages in Part 3.

Knowing how the printing press worked can help you understand the features you see in an early printed book. Repeated errors in headlines, upside-down blocks of type, overlaying red and black print, for example, are all extant textual clues of a long-past process of skeleton forms, bearing type, and incorrectly registered printing. And such errors can be clues as to not only how one book was produced, but to a system of book production. Randall McLeod (writing as Random Cloud) has used the impressions left by bearing type to identify books that were printed concurrently, for instance. Adrian Weiss looks more broadly at the bibliographical evidence of presswork in Thomas Middleton's *The triumphs of honor and vertue* (STC 17900) and deduces how Nicolas Okes printed the pageant and the workflow of his shop.

This sort of work—moving from looking at bibliographic features to deducing press operations—has opened up many larger possibilities for study. For economic and labor historians, the practices of the early modern print shop can illuminate working conditions, guild organization, and social relations. If you're looking to understand the differences between manual production and industrial mass production, the details and processes of printing are a useful place to start. Even if your focus is limited to book trade in the Renaissance, you won't be able to comprehend the market and its forces without an understanding of printing. And, of course, textual scholars who are editing texts for modern readers—indeed, the recognition that such texts need some sort of editorial intervention—rely on an understanding of the printing process to be able to recognize errors and make changes.

Corrections and Changes

Presses often have someone act as a proofreader—after the forme is set, an impression is printed, read over for corrections, and any changes marked onto the printed sheet. (The system of marks that we use today in proofreading is largely the same as was used then.) The compositor then picks out pieces of type and replaces them with the corrected reading, which is then locked up and returned to the pressmen. Even after that point, the corrected forme sometimes is marked up with several revises.

But even with such proofreading, changes might need to be made during a print run. Sometimes errors are missed, sometimes errors are introduced during an earlier change, sometimes editorial decisions, censorship, or other interventions require an alteration of the text. Early printers had a range of methods they used to make or indicate such changes.

Stop-press Changes

One of the benefits of movable type is that it can be reset at any point during the printing process. If an error is noticed during a print run, and it is deemed important enough to stop the presses and correct it, pieces of type can be picked out and replaced while the forme is still on the press stone. If it's a simple change—adjusting a turned letter or swapping out a word for another of the same length—there is often nothing in the end result to indicate there's been a change unless you carefully compare it to other copies (a process known as collating).

Collating your book

If you are editing or otherwise carefully studying a text, you might need to identify any stop-press changes made during its production. You can do this by hand, putting two copies side by side and looking at each one word by word (what Randall McLeod calls the Wimbledon method). But there are various optical collators that are not only faster, but that also make visible any adjustments to the setting. The first of these, the Hinman collator developed by Charlton Hinman and used in his study of the First Folio, is now rarely used. More recent collators developed by McLeod and Carter Hailey have the advantage of being portable. These devices take advantage of the user's natural binocular vision by having each eye look at a separate copy of the book; as the brain tries to make them conform into one image, any changes seem to jiggle or float.

But sometimes changing one word or phrase requires adjusting the entire line or even adjacent ones. Because the page being changed still needs to end in the same place (so that subsequent pages don't have to be reset), the compositor will sometimes adjust spacing or spelling in order to have the new type fit smoothly. Once the forme is unlocked for the changes, however, it's possible for other changes to be accidentally introduced—a letter can be unintentionally removed and replaced incorrectly, a line can pie and be scrambled when it is reset. These more complex changes are often also invisible unless copies are compared against each other. But sometimes they leave readily visible evidence behind, such as a page with 31 lines of text abutting the direction line, rather than a 30-line page that has a space between the main text block and the direction line.

Errata Lists

Sometimes a list of errors will be used to indicate to the reader that there are errors in the printed text. These errata lists are usually found at the end of the preliminaries or at the end of the book. Often the errata list will be prefaced by an apology from the printer for the mistakes and an invitation to the reader to correct them herself. The precise form of the list itself varies, but typically it includes a page or leaf number and the corrected reading. Some errata lists identify both the error and the correction, using language like "p. 28 read *conversed* for *converted*" to indicate that the mistaken "converted" should be corrected to "conversed." Other errata notes provide only the page or gathering and the correction, leaving the reader to identify the precise error.

An errata list may also be printed onto a slip of paper and pasted in to the book. Such a slip may only be present in some copies, not all.

There is only one known copy of John Donne's 1612 *Anniversaries* (STC 7023) that contains the errata slip, for instance. And some copies of Robert Glover's 1608 *Nobilitas politica vel civilis* (STC 11922) have a 30-line errata slip pasted over the original 14-line errata list!

Based on the annotations of surviving books, some readers followed the requests of the printer to mark the corrections. Other books, however, don't show evidence of readers having noted the changes.

Cancels

Another method of making changes to a book is to insert or paste in printed corrections. These corrections are known as cancels, with the replaced text the cancelland. Sometimes changes are complex enough that an entire leaf will be printed, with the intention that the changed leaf will replace the original one. In order to insert a single leaf, the original leaf is cut out of the gathering and the new leaf pasted onto the stub left behind by the original. A leaf can also be inserted by sewing it into the gathering; where that is the case, there will be a stub from the new leaf showing where the conjugate leaf would normally be.

The insertion of cancel leaves is done at the binding stage, after the sheets have been gathered, with the cancelland typically indicated by a slash through the leaf. The cancel (usually printed with a signature mark to indicate where it belonged) is then inserted by attaching it to the stub of the removed cancelland. Sometimes, however, a binder missed the slashed cancelland or inserted the cancel without removing the cancelland.

Figure 24 The sixth leaf in this gathering is an inserted cancel, with the stub of the leaf showing between the first two leaves of the gathering. The fourth leaf is a cancel that has been pasted on to the stub left behind after the original cancelland was removed. Based on a sketch by the author.

Cancels weren't only for entire leaves, but could also be used for paragraphs or words or even letters. In those cases, a cancel slip would be printed and then pasted in over the section that needed to be changed. In many cases, the pasted-in slip is fairly obvious, since you can see the edges of the slip, but it was also possible for the slip to be done carefully enough for it not to be immediately apparent. Looking at the leaf through a light, however, will reveal the darker area where there are two layers of paper.

Why does it Matter?

The process of how changes and corrections were made to hand-press books has been central to understanding the relationships between different texts and identifying which state or edition precedes another. Recognizing that a book might be made up of sheets in various states—some changed and some not—means that textual scholars interested in identifying the correct text must trace not the evolution of the whole book, but the changes across specific formes.

The details of changes sometimes provide some insight into who worked in print shops. John Stow's 1561 edition of Chaucer's works is in two states (STC 5075 and 5076) with multiple differences between the two, including the presence of woodcuts (STC 5075) and changes to the text. Some of those textual changes, interestingly, require a familiarity with Middle English in order to recognize the original errors (see Joseph Dane and Seth Lerer's examination of this edition for elucidation about this and the volume as a whole).

If most authors were not involved in the production and correction of their books, there are also some clear examples of authorial investment in the process. Mary Wroth's copy of her 1621 romance *Urania* shows her manuscript annotations correcting the text (STC 26051; now held at the University of Pennsylvania, shelfmark Folio PR2399. W7 C68 1621). A more complex example is that of Augustine Vincent's 1623 *A discouerie of errours in the first edition of the catalogue of nobility, published by Raphe Brooke, Yorke Herald, 1619* (STC 24756). Vincent's book is, as the title says, an account of the mistakes made in Brooke's work of heraldry (STC 3832). Given Vincent's insistence on correcting errors, it should be no surprise that he was careful to ensure that his own work was free from mistakes. Not only did Vincent seem to review the proofs, he sent proofs to the historian John Selden, who replied with corrections. The result is a book that, paradoxically, looks particularly careless as it incorporates corrections via nearly all such means: an errata list, cancel leaves, pasted-in slips, and even overprinting (printing corrections on top of the already-printed sheet).

The changes themselves can also be revealing of religious, political, and societal fissures, with one part of a text being dangerous enough to call attention to (or being perceived to do so) possibly punitive authorities. Tracing the types of changes made in response to church objections highlights the most contentious areas of theology. The censorship of texts that are deemed licentious reveals what types of sexual behavior are dangerously beyond limits, as opposed to tolerated or endorsed. Looking for where texts have been changed and how printers responded to the pressures of both corrections and censorship brings bibliography and social history together in a fruitful conversation.

Illustrations

Depending on whether they are woodcuts or intaglio prints, illustrations in early printed books can be printed at the same time as the text or printed separately on a different type of press. Being able to identify the techniques used to make and print book illustrations can help us understand the material features of a book and the broader book trade.

Woodcuts

Woodcuts are a type of relief printing: the part of the surface that stands in relief is the part that prints on the paper. (Hand-press type is also relief printing.)

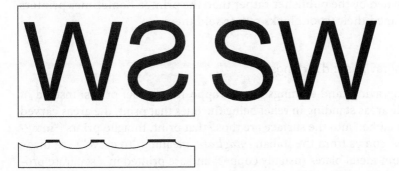

Figure 25 In relief printing, the white spaces are carved away, leaving the parts to be printed raised, as on the left; below is a cross-section of the foot of the block, showing the raised parts. The woodblock is a mirror image of what is printed, shown on the right. Based on a sketch by the author.

The first step is carving the image into a block of wood—typically along the grain of a plank cut to a standard height that is the same as the body of a piece of type. The desired image is typically drawn onto the woodblock, or onto a piece of paper that is pasted onto the wood, and then the white areas (the negative spaces) of the image are carved out of the block, leaving the areas that should print standing in relief. Just as with type, the picture will be printed as the mirror image of what's on the woodblock; for many images, it won't matter which way it prints, but letters, of course, would have to be reversed. If necessary, areas of the woodblock can be removed and replaced with a new plug of wood to alter the image.

After the block is carved, it can be printed at the same time as the text of the book on the same common press. Since the block has the same height as the type, the surface to be printed is even and it is generally handled in the same way a page of type is. Once the compositor has finished his work, the type and the woodblock are locked into a forme together and printed as usual. Multiple woodblocks can appear on the same page, or a single large woodblock could make up an entire page. If an image is intended to spread across a page opening (that is, a pair of facing pages), it needs to be printed with two separate and carefully aligned blocks.

Woodblocks can be reused in the same book (although not, of course, in the same forme, since a single block cannot be in two places at once) and in different books. Some woodblocks are generic details—borders, initial letters, tail pieces—that a printer owns and uses as he sees fit. Others are more specifically designed for certain works—plants for herbals, for example—and might be owned by the publisher rather than the printer. Sometimes printers loaned their woodblocks out or sold them.

Engravings and Etchings

Engravings and etchings are the opposite of relief prints: instead of the areas standing in relief being the ones that print, the areas carved or etched into the surface are those that print. Intaglio prints ("intaglio" comes from the Italian *intagliare*, meaning "to carve") are made from metal plates (usually copper) and are printed in a separate process from the text on a rolling press.

Although engravings and etchings print according to the same principles, the process of creating the image on the copper plates differs. Engraved plates are made by carving lines out of the copper plate with a sharp tool called a burin. The burin has a v-shaped point, and

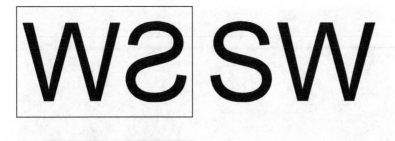

Figure 26 In intaglio printing, the areas to be printed are cut into the surface of the plate and the ink forced into them; the cross-piece of the foot of the plate shows how the letters are cut in and filled with ink. The plate is the reverse image of the printed letters, shown on the right. Based on a sketch by the author.

the deeper it is pushed into the plate, the wider the groove it leaves. By altering the pressure on the burin, the engraver can allow some lines to print darker than others. Engravers would often lightly scratch the image they were creating onto the surface of the copper to serve as guide lines for the deeper cuts.

In etched plates, the grooves are made by acid burning the plate. The blank plate is warmed and covered with a layer of wax or other protective varnish (called the ground). Once the wax is hardened, it is impervious to acid. The etcher can then remove the areas of wax where grooves are wanted, leaving the wax in place where white spaces are desired. The wax is fairly easy to scrape away—easier than carving out copper—and so the artist can draw freehand on the plate to create the image he wants. Once the image is carved into the wax, the plate is dipped into an acid bath. The longer the acid is in contact with the copper, the deeper its bite. By letting some areas be exposed longer than others—reapplying the ground to already exposed sections to protect them—the printmaker can vary the tones of the image that will result. With both engraving and etching, if the image needs to be changed, the metal can be pounded smooth and the image can be redone.

Once the plate is ready, the same process is used for printing both engraved and etched images. The copper plate is warmed and ink is carefully and firmly worked over the plate, making sure that it is pushed down into the grooves. After the plate has been inked, its surface is then cleaned of ink, leaving behind only the ink in the grooves.

Since it takes a great amount of pressure to push the paper into the plate's grooves to pull up the ink, the press for this is quite different

Figure 27 "The Invention of Copper Engraving" from the series *Nova Reperta*. On the left is a rolling press, with the printer exerting great force to turn the rollers. In the center, two men are preparing a plate for printing, warming and wiping off the ink. In the background on the right is a man flattening a copper plate in preparation for engraving, while on the left another man is hanging prints to dry. Public domain image made available by the Metropolitan Museum of Art (49.95.870(10)).

A note about colored prints

The overwhelming majority of book illustrations in this period were printed in black ink on white paper. In some categories of books, however, coloring prints by hand was frequently done; in atlases and herbals, maps and illustrations of plants were often colored. Hand-coloring was usually done professionally, sometimes using stencils, sometimes freehand. (For information about printing text in red ink, see the note in "Printing" in this part.)

from the one used to print type and woodcuts. Instead of the flat platen used in a common press (which distributes pressure across its entire surface), a rolling press squeezes the paper and plate between two large rollers, concentrating the pressure at a single line of contact and forcing the paper down into the plate's grooves. The result is an image with lines that are slightly raised (since they have been embossed into the plate) and with a raised mark at the edges where the copper plate has been pushed into the paper.

As with woodblocks, plates can be reused in the same book or in other books. They were more typically owned by the publisher than by the printer, but were also sometimes traded or sold.

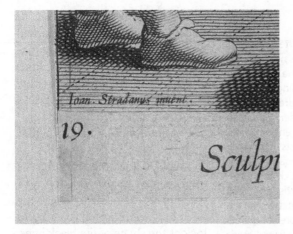

Figure 28 In this detail of the lower left corner of the print, you can see the platemark left by the force used to press the paper into the copper plate. The inscription "Ioan. Stradanus inuent." refers to the artist Jan van der Straet, who drew the picture that was the basis for this engraving. Public domain image made available by the Metropolitan Museum of Art (49.95.870(10).

How to Identify a Print

So how can you recognize whether a print is woodcut or intaglio? The first thing to look for is a plate mark. All intaglio prints are made from plates that undergo great pressure from the rolling press, leaving behind a raised edge where the unpressed paper meets the area flattened by the plate. Sometimes the resulting print will be trimmed so that the plate marks are cut off. But often the edges of the plate are close enough to the image that they can't be trimmed away. Since woodblocks only print what's in relief, the edges of the blocks don't leave raised marks. (They can sometimes leave inked marks.) If you can find a plate mark, you're looking at an intaglio print.

If you don't see a plate mark, there are other signs to look for. One is the shape of the lines. In woodcuts, black lines are created by carving out white spaces around them. This means that they are often not quite straight; when you look at them magnified, you can see that the edges of the lines, or the lines themselves, look a bit wobbly. In intaglio prints, black lines are created by removing the line itself; the resulting lines have crisper edges.

You can also look at the white spaces in areas that are crosshatched. Crosshatching is a technique of using intersecting black lines to create shaded areas, an easy way to create levels of darkness between black and white before the ability to create gray areas. In intaglio prints, the black lines are carved first in one direction, and then again

Signing prints

Engravings and etchings are often signed by their makers, but that person is not necessarily who we would think of as the original artist. In the illustration of the rolling press used in this section, the artist who drew the original picture was Jan van der Straet, or Stradanus; the person who engraved the plate was Jan Collaert. The artists in these different roles might have their names signed on the print with Latin terms such as "invenit" ("designed") for the original artist and "fecit" ("made") for the engraver or etcher. A list of commonly used terms and abbreviations can be found in Anthony Griffiths's useful guide, *Prints and Printmaking*.

running across the first set of lines. The resulting area is marked by black lines and tiny white diamonds in between where the lines cross. In relief printing, those tiny white spaces are carved out, and as a result, they often are not precise diamonds but rougher shapes.

If you've identified a print as intaglio, you might wish to know whether it was made by engraving or etching. Here, again, you want to look at the shape of the black lines. Since engraving is made by pushing a burin into the metal plate, the resulting lines have smooth edges and pointed ends where the burin lifts up. They also typically vary in width, swelling in the middle as the burin is pushed deeper, and becoming thinner at the ends as the pressure is lifted. Etched lines, on the other hand, have rounded ends, are a bit wobblier, and have the same width throughout the line. (Think about the difference between pushing through metal and carving away wax—the former makes steadier grooves, since it takes a lot of force to alter the metal, while the ease of carving away wax means it reveals slight changes in direction.)

Why does it Matter?

Understanding the physical processes of how prints were made reveals what illustrations can tell us about book production and circulation. One key point is that copper-plate illustrations require a separate rolling press for printing. And because using a rolling press was a specialized skill, such illustrations had to be sent to a different printing house, making such books more complex to produce than those that used only a common press. Some books included full-page intaglio prints that could be made at the same time as the text of a book, albeit at a different shop, and then joined together during the volume's gathering and binding. In those cases, plate numbers are included on the illustrations to easily identify them and often there may be a note to the binder appended to the text that says where they are to be inserted. (The paper used in such full-page intaglio printing was usually supplied by the printer, not the publisher, and so was a different stock than that used for the text of a book.)

But sometimes an intaglio print appeared on the same page as letterpress text. In those cases, the book would be printed with a blank space left for the illustration. Then the sheets would be sent over to the shop with the rolling press, and carefully laid out so that the blank space in the text aligned with the copper plate of the image. The resulting sheet, if done well, has the image (and its plate marks) fit within the space waiting for it. But such alignment was not always so successful, and sometimes you can see plates that slightly overlap or are slightly askew from the text. (Sometimes you even find prints that are upside down!)

Because including intaglio prints required contracting with a second printing shop, it was generally more complex than printing a work with no illustrations or with woodblocks. The economic ramifications of this have not been well studied—bibliographers have typically been primarily interested in text, not image. But it seems likely that adding intaglio prints to a hand-press book added to the production costs of the book. Roger Gaskell estimates that adding one newly made plate to a 500-copy print run of a book raises machining costs by 10% and overall production costs by 5%.

Illustrations can be used to help identify how old a text is by considering how worn the pictures are. Because woodblocks and copper plates were separate physical items from a book's text, they could be reused in other books and they often circulated well beyond their first use. The natural wear and tear on a block or plate can help researchers date when an item was printed: if a block developed a crack during the course of its life, the visibility of and changes to that crack can suggest when it was used. While copper plates didn't develop cracks, the depth of their grooves did change over their lifetime, especially between editions, as Blair Hedges has shown, since each time a plate was polished for storage its grooves became shallower from the erosion of the plate's surface, and the printed lines thinner.

Binding

Binding a book is a separate process done by people who specialize in the work, sometimes shortly after a book is printed and sometimes much later. Since the cost of binding is borne by the person who ordered it, and since bound volumes take up more room to store than gathered sheets, sellers typically only have a few copies bound at a time, in case a customer wants to buy an already bound book. Other copies are kept stored in sheets, waiting to be bound and sold, or sold as is so that the buyer can bind them according to her preference.

The question of if and when a book is bound is related in part to its size. Smaller works of a handful of sheets are often sold and kept in a form that is lightly sewn together (stab-stitched). The binder takes a needle and thread and passes it through the whole block of sheets near the edge of the fold so that it runs through the inner margins of the leaves. It's a quick and effective way of keeping a short book together. Of course, a stab-stitched book doesn't lie flat, and it's not a technique that works well with larger volumes, which are too thick to sew through in a single pass.

Buyers might keep their books as stitched, or have a few bound together into a single volume. Stab-stitched books could also have paper or vellum wrappers. The wrappers used could be a rough wrapping paper, manuscript or printed paper waste, plain vellum, or old

Figure 29 A copy of the 1634 edition of *Richard II* (STC 22313) with the stab-stitch structure highlighted; notice the untrimmed edges, especially visible at the bottom, and the multiple gatherings. Public domain image made available by the Harry Ransom Center (PFORZ 896).

bits of vellum manuscripts. Paper wrappers were used in Italy in the 16th century, and in France, Germany, and other parts of the continent thereafter, but didn't become part of English binding practices until the 18th century.

If a book is to be sewn into a binding, the binder first checks the order of the sheets and inserts any required plates. The gathered block of sheets is then hammered flat and placed onto a sewing frame.

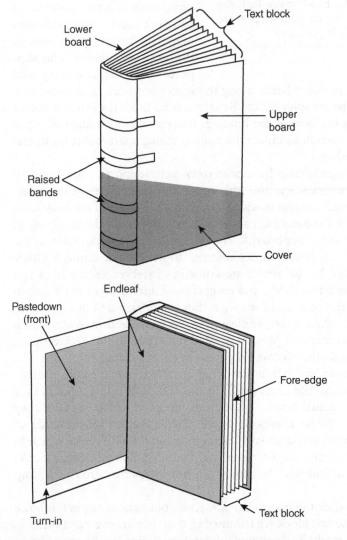

Figure 30 Some key binding elements. Based on a sketch by the author.

False bands

Raised bands on the spines of books once came from an integral part of the sewing structure. But as binding techniques changed to cheaper and faster methods, sewing onto supports was eliminated. Often the binder would still include raised bands along the spine to create the illusion of a more robust binding. These false bands might look like raised bands from the outside, but they are not a part of the sewing structure.

There the gatherings (lying horizontally) are sewn onto supports (thongs or cords running vertically), with the thread passing through the center of the fold and then wrapping around the support. There is a wide range of ways in which the sewing can be done, with different patterns of stitching and with different materials for and placement of the sewing supports. The supports could be outside the fold (resulting in raised bands along the spine) or placed in slots cut into the folds (so the spine is flat). Sewing is what holds the leaves together and forms the core of the binding. It's typically not visible after the binding is complete, unless the book is falling apart, but it is integral to any binding.

Once the gatherings have been sewn onto supports, a few leaves of blank paper are sewn onto the upper and lower parts of the book. These protect the text block and reinforce the joints of the boards. In many cases, the outermost sheets will be pasted onto the inner side of the upper and lower boards. That leaf is known as a pastedown; the conjugate leaf is sometimes referred to as the free endleaf. Other leaves added by the binder are known as flyleaves. (Sometimes you will see the terms flyleaf and endleaf used interchangeably; it's often best to check yourself to see what they are referring to in a book.) In addition to blank paper, endleaves might be made from plain vellum or recycled manuscripts and printed materials; in the 17th century, marbled and other decorated papers begin to be used.

Next, if there are to be boards, they are attached to the book. Boards are what make the covers stiff. In the 15th and 16th centuries they were often actual boards made from pieces of wood, but later they were likely to be sheets of paper glued together (pasteboard) or pressed together (pulpboard). Sometimes, in the 18th century, boards were made from pulped ropes and hemp (millboard). Some books were not bound with boards at all, but instead covered with limp vellum.

Usually after the boards are attached (but sometimes before), the edges of the text block are trimmed so that they are even and smooth. The edges might be decorated by staining, gilding, gauffering (cutting designs into them), speckling, or marbling. In the middle of the 17th century, fore-edges were sometimes decorated with pictures, either painted when the book was closed or when the pages were slightly fanned, so that the image was hidden when the book was closed.

Finally, if desired, the boards are covered and decorated. There was a wide range of materials used in bindings, although animal skins were the most prevalent. Some choices signaled regional preferences: blind-tooled alum pigskin, for example, was often used in Germany and northern Europe. Calfskin was frequently used as a material that was both durable and not expensive and that could be decorated if desired; books bought bound from the bookseller were usually covered in calf. Goatskin (often called morocco leather, although it wasn't necessarily from Morocco) was more expensive than calf, but could be dyed strong colors. Sheepskin was a cheap, if not long-lasting, alternative. Vellum and parchment could be used over boards or as a limp cover.

Books could also be covered in fancier materials like velvet, embroidered cloth, or silver. Velvet was not durable but could be used for special books, such as prayer books and bibles. Embroidered bindings were typically used for small devotional books; they were popular in the early decades of the 17th century. The embroidery was usually done professionally, often following patterns depicting flowers or biblical scenes.

Leather covers could be left plain or decorated. Sometimes a binding was decorated by using hot metal tools leaving impressions (tooled); the resulting designs could be left as is (blind tooling) or filled with gold leaf (gilt tooled). Bindings were often decorated primarily to look pretty, with borders and patterns; sometimes they included an owner's initials or coat of arms. Bindings could also have leather and metal clasps or cloth ties

A note about spine titles

Books in the early part of this period were usually stored lying down, in chests, or shelved spine in; only in the middle of the 16th century did they start to shift to being stored as we shelve them today, with the spine out. For this reason, sometimes you see title or author information marked on the fore-edge of books; spine lettering and labels weren't common until the 18th century.

Chained bindings

Institutional libraries in this period often kept their books chained to shelves or desks so that readers didn't walk off with them. Some chained libraries still survive intact, and some books with chains can be found in other collections. But chains were more often removed from bindings once they were no longer needed—it's hard to store a binding with chains without damaging the book or the volumes around it. If the rest of the binding has been left intact, you might see evidence of a former chain in two large holes left near the edge of the board from where it had been attached.

attached to keep the book closed. Generally speaking, English and French books attached their clasps so they hung down from the upper board, with the catch on the lower; other countries reversed the order, with the clasp on the lower and the catch on the upper. Books might also have metal furniture attached to protect the binding—corner pieces and circular bosses. While such furniture was originally intended to keep the covers away from damaging surfaces, it later shifted to a primarily decorative function.

Sometimes an owner would choose to have a group of different texts bound together to make a single volume. Such books are known, following the German, as "sammelbände" ("sammelband" in the singular) or "bound withs." Early owners might choose to group related texts together in a single volume, such as a collection of playbooks or works about Protestantism. (See "Differentiating Between Early and Later Characteristics" in Part 5 on how such early bindings were often replaced with bindings that separated texts.)

Figure 31 An embroidered dos-à-dos binding from around 1610 of a New Testament and a Book of Psalms, bound so that held one way, the NT is on top, and the other, the Psalter. Image made available by the Folger Shakespeare Library under a CC BY-SA 4.0 license (STC 2907).

Books could also be bound together in a manner that allowed the reader to easily find the first page of a text, a technique usually used for small devotional texts. Dos-à-dos bindings (that is, back-to-back) bind together two texts so that they share a lower board, which is in the middle of the volume, and the two exposed boards are the upper boards for each text. For instance, if you hold a dos-à-dos book in your hand and open it, you'll find the start of the New Testament; turn the book over, head to tail, and open it and you'll find the start of a Psalter.

Some books have survived without having been bound. Unsold stock, for instance, might remain in a warehouse in sheets until it becomes a collector's item. Of course, sheets unprotected by bindings are vulnerable to damage. They are even more susceptible to being reused as scrap paper in other books: bindings often incorporated waste paper to make pasteboards, spine guards, or pastedowns. In fact, there are manuscript and printed texts that we only know of today because they were accidentally preserved in bindings.

Many of the hand-press books that we now see in libraries have been rebound by later owners. As a general rule, the more prestigious the work, the more likely it is to be in a 19th- or 20th-century binding. Only a tiny portion of the surviving 235 copies of Shakespeare's First Folio (STC 22273), for example, are in 17th-century bindings. But copies of the multi-language parallel-column phrasebooks known as Berlaimonts, like the one we looked at in the Introduction, often remain in their contemporary bindings. Dating bindings can be tricky work, but some guidelines can be found in Part 5.

Why does it Matter?

Bindings can help us understand how early readers used and thought of their books. Dos-à-dos bindings emphasize the close relationship between how the New Testament and the Book of Psalms were used; folios with heavy furniture suggest volumes that were kept on lecterns. Sometimes bindings can point to ways of thinking about books that we would otherwise miss. Whereas today we tend to see a strict division between manuscript and print, medieval and Renaissance sammelbände that bound together both forms of text suggest that their users did not see that division. The work of Jeffrey Todd Knight suggests the myriad things we can learn from how books were bound and later disbound.

Our understanding of the book trade can also be illuminated by considering when, where, and how books were bound. Since books were bound where they were sold, not where they were printed, sometimes a contemporary binding that shows regional characteristics can reveal the circulation of books. The changes to the structure of bindings over time is connected to the rising popularity of printed books: as the rate of publications grew, bindings shifted to structures that were faster and cheaper to make.

Part 3
On the Page

Not only does the process of making hand-press books differ from how books are made today, many of the features that you see on the pages of old books are unfamiliar. There can be unexpected words, letters, and numbers at the foot of the page; title pages might not be there or they might seem inordinately full of information; and even the ways words are written can be unfamiliar. Such aspects of hand-press books are as important for understanding them as the ways in which they're made.

In this part of the guide, we'll look at some of the things we see on and as pages in early printed books. It is organized into discrete sections, presented alphabetically. Many of these features are best understood by seeing examples of them; while some illustrations are included in this guide, more can be found at your rare books library or online at Early Printed Books (http://www.earlyprintedbooks.com). Resources for further study are included in the section of Appendix 1 devoted to "On the Page" but you can find additional resources in the general and cataloging sections.

Advertisements

Sometimes books will include advertisements for other books sold by the bookseller. These are primarily a feature of books printed in Britain and North America in the 17th and 18th centuries, and they usually appear on integral but otherwise blank leaves at the end of book sections (most often at the end of the book itself) or on unused spaces such as the verso of a title page. For example, in the last gathering of the 1660 octavo *Aminta* (Wing T172), the text ends on the third leaf (sig. L3v), followed by three leaves of advertisements for other books sold by its publisher, John Starkey (sigs L4r-L7v), and a final

Studying Early Printed Books 1450–1800: A Practical Guide, First Edition. Sarah Werner.
© 2019 Sarah Werner. Published 2019 by John Wiley & Sons Ltd.

blank leaf (sig. L8). Around 1661, the play *Philaster* (Wing B1599) was sold by William Leake with ads for books included on the verso of the title page (sig. A1v) and on the next leaf, just below the dramatis personae (sig. A2v) and before the text begins on sig. B1r.

Advertisements weren't only for books, or on interior leaves. The brief mid-18th-century fiction *Noble revenge; or, The King of Spain confederate with a cobbler* includes in the title-page imprint statement, "printed and sold by T. Bailey, Ship and Crown, Leaden-hall-street; where tradesmens bills are printed at the letterpress and off copper-plates. Where Maredant's Anti-scorbutic Drops are sold at six shilling the bottle, which cures the most inveterate scurvy, leprosy, &c. likewise to be had at Mr. Norton's music shop, in Drury Lane, near Long Acre" (ESTC T505419).

Such ads can be useful in tracing the dates and printers of books published without that information in their imprint. *The Lilliputian letter-writer* (ESTC N504266) is conjectured to have been published in 1795 since that work is listed in an advertisement for "publications for the instruction and amusement of young people" included in a different book sold by the same bookseller that year. The printer and seller of the children's book *The history of Prince Abdul, and the princess Selima* (ESTC 505804) is identified as John Luffman by the presence of an advertisement for his books at the back of the volume.

Such lists assist in bibliographic evidence, but they can also be used to study the book trade and how books were classified. If a bookseller regularly advertises his wares, you can trace when new stock appears. And since such ads often categorize books according to genre or other schemes, they can serve as a window onto how early modern sellers and readers thought of such classifications. (Adam G. Hooks's work has used bookseller's ads in these ways to explore printed English drama.) Particularly intriguing, and frustrating, are bookseller's ads that provide evidence of publications that are now otherwise lost.

Of course, advertisements circulated as texts in and of themselves. Auction catalogs and advertisements for theater and music performances were circulated in print. Publishers also circulated prospectuses for books looking for subscribers. And, of course, title pages themselves could be displayed as advertisements.

Alphabet and Abbreviations

One of the first things that readers of hand-press books notice is that not only do they spell words differently than we do today, they do not even seem to use the alphabet the way we do. The most perplexing to new readers is what to our eyes appear as misused "u"s, "v"s, "i"s, and "j"s, along with the unfamiliar "ſ." Words like "vnder," "deuout," "iuſtice," and "ſallow" are easy to stumble over. Practice makes perfect in reading smoothly, but it helps to understand why these words are written like this.

The Latin alphabet used in Europe in the hand-press period treated "u" and "v" as alternate graphical forms of a single letter and "i" and "j" as alternate forms of a single letter. Similarly, the letter "s" existed in two shapes, a short "s" and the now obsolete long-s, "ſ." The alternate forms are not used randomly, but follow standard practices. The sharp "v" is used at the start of words, while the round "u" is used in the middle and end of words; the short "i" is used at the start and in the middle of words, while the long "j" is used at the end of words; and the long "ſ" is used at the start and in the middle of words, while the short "s" is used at the end.

The dominance of Latin, which did not use the letter "w," meant that some fonts did not always include that sort, or enough of the sort for languages like English, which has a higher frequency of "w" usage than French. When a single "w" wasn't available, printers substituted two "v"s in its place. (English speakers say "double-you" for this letter, but French speakers, for example, say "double-vay.")

There were also some residual letterforms and abbreviations from medieval scribes that carried over into printing. One of those is the use of the letter thorn, "þ," which was also written as a "y." In printing, the use of "y" to stand in for "þ" was used sometimes instead of the more contemporary "th" when abbreviating: "y^e" is another way of writing "the" and "y^t" an abbreviation of "that." (The thorn has disappeared from our alphabet, visible only in the "Ye Olde Shoppe" type signs.) The use of superscript letters generally indicates an abbreviation: "y^{or}" for "your" or "w^{ch}" for "which." Other abbreviations that continue to be used in print include the use of macrons or tildes to indicate an omitted letter, usually an "m" or "n": "heavē" as "heaven."

When transcribing a text that uses the 23-letter alphabet or abbreviations, it's generally best to be consistent and to provide a note to your reader as to how you've proceeded. You can choose to regularize the spelling completely, using u/v, i/j, and s/ſ according to modern usage and spelling out all abbreviations. You can also choose to keep the originals as much as possible, using the u/v and i/j letters as in the original. (Generally, a ſ is transcribed as "s" since most typefaces today do not include the long-s letterform.) You will sometimes see, when reading transcriptions or modern editions of

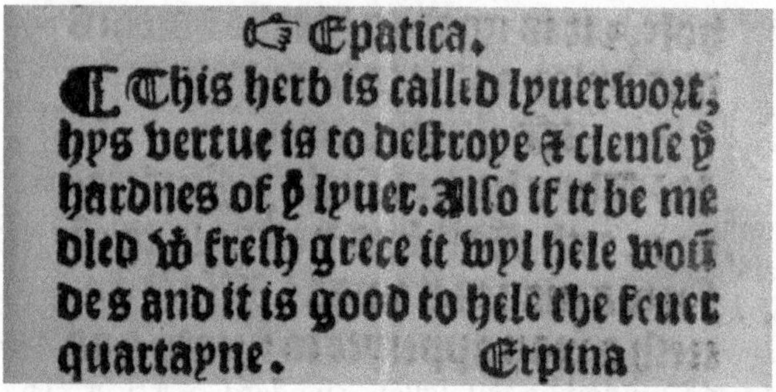
☞ Epatica.
¶ This herb is called lyuerwort,
hys vertue is to destroye & clense ẏ
hardnes of ẏ lyuer. Also if it be me
dled ẘ fresh grece it wyl hele wou͞
des and it is good to hele the feuer
quartayne. Erpina

Figure 32 An account of the herb hepatica from *A Boke of the propreties of herbes called an herball*, printed in blackletter around 1542. From a public domain image made available by the US National Library of Medicine (WZ 240 M927m 1546, sig. C7r).

early texts, that italics have been used to indicate when abbreviations have been expanded, a method that both preserves the form of the original and makes it easier for modern reading.

The passage in Figure 32 is from a 1552 edition of Bancke's Herbal (STC 13175.15a) and describes the properties of a plant called hepatica, or liverwort, which was used to treat liver ailments and wounds.

What follows is a semi-diplomatic transcription that keeps the original letterforms and expands abbreviations by noting them in italics. (A diplomatic transcription or edition is one that strives to reproduce a document exactly as it is, from spelling to layout to material features. This is semi-diplomatic in that it strives to represent how the words are on the page, but doesn't preserve other aspects of the document.)

> Epatica.
> This herb is called lyuerwort, hys vertue is to destroye & clense *th*e hardnes of *th*e lyuer. Also if it be medled w*ith* fresh grece it wyl hele wou*n*des and it is good to hele the feuer quartayne.

Such a transcription style gives a sense of the original spelling of the passage, but it isn't particularly easy to read, especially for those not used to early modern English. You might choose instead to regularize i/j and u/v according to our usage and to expand the abbreviations without noting them:

> Epatica.
> This herb is called lyverwort, hys vertue is to destroye and clense the hardnes of the lyver. Also if it be medled with fresh grece it wyl hele woundes and it is good to hele the fever quartayne.

You could also choose to modernize the spelling and punctuation, as below.

> Hepatica.
> This herb is called liverwort. His virtue is to destroy and cleanse the hardness of the liver. Also, if it be muddled with fresh grease, it will heal wounds, and it is good to heal the fever quartain.

Depending on your project, any of these options could be the correct one.

Blanks

Blank leaves at the beginning and end of a text block are easily lost over time, either torn off accidentally or removed during binding or rebinding. Interior blank pages are typically found on the versos of title pages and plates and at the end of sections (especially if it coincides with the end of a gathering). They can also appear for less common reasons, such as the result of poor casting off, as part of an inserted pair of conjugate leaves, or from space being left for text or an illustration that wasn't added. Sometimes on these blank pages there will be text along the lines of "nihil hic deest" ("nothing is lacking") to indicate the blank is deliberate, much like today's "this page intentionally left blank." See the note about bearing type in "Printing" in Part 2 for information about how blank spaces on pages are set.

It's easy to overlook blank pages if you're only focused on a text, but they are an integral part of the printing and binding processes. (Of course, these printer's blanks are not to be confused with binder's blanks, or the flyleaves that are added by the binder to the text block.)

Dates

The imprint dates provided in colophons and title pages range in difficulty from more to less easy to understand (more on imprints can be found in this part in "Imprint Statements"). Colophons might provide the exact day that a book finished being printed, but sometimes in terms of a monarch's reign or a saint's day, and often in roman numbers, not the arabic ones we use. The system of roman numbers used isn't always the same that we use. And to top it off, English and continental calendars didn't always agree on what date it was or when the year changed.

William Caxton's edition of John Gower's poem *Confessio amatis* (STC 12142) ends with a colophon reading "Enprynted at Westmestre: By me Willyam Caxton, and fynysshed the ij day of Septembre the fyrst yere of the regne of Kyng Richard the Thyrd, the yere of our lord a thousand, CCCC, lxxxxiij." The information here seems straightforward: the book was finished on September 2 in the first year of the reign of Richard III, that is, the year 1493. But Richard III's reign started in 1483. So which date is correct? Presumably the regnal year—adding an extra "x" to the roman date is an easy mistake to make, but getting confused between the first year and the tenth year of your monarch's reign is not. (Note that the date follows the i/j conventions discussed in "Alphabet": the final "i" is written as "j.")

Catalog records usually will provide roman dates in arabic numerals, but it's useful to be able to read them yourself. (If you're unfamiliar with using roman numerals, there are plenty of explanations online.) There are some differences and regional variations to be aware of. Numbers that we would typically write as "iv" or "ix" sometimes are written out as "iiii" and "viiii." While "M" is typically used for 1000 and D as 500, some imprints use "cIↄ" for 1000 and "cI" as 500. (The "cIↄ" is an approximation of the Greek Φ, which was used by Romans as a symbol representing 1000. "cI" is obviously half of a Φ and therefore 500.)

Sometimes a book printed near the end of a calendar year will be dated the following calendar year. This isn't an attempt to deceive the buyer, but a way of avoiding making the book appear out of date before it's even been sold (publishers do the same thing today). But the day on which the year changed is also confusing: in England, the legal year changed on March 25 (Lady Day, or the Feast of Annunciation), so that the day after December 31, 1611, was January 1, 1611, and the day after March 24, 1611, was March 25, 1612. This practice was phased out of use in Britain in the middle of the 17th century; most continental countries stopped changing the legal year on March 25 in the 15th century.

England also continued to follow the Julian calendar until 1752, long after Catholic countries had changed to the Gregorian calendar in 1582, when a change imposed by Pope Gregory skipped the calendar ahead 10 days in order to realign it with the solar cycle. The 10-day lag between Old Style and New Style dating will rarely come up but is helpful to know about (and is a useful reminder of the many divisions between Catholic and Protestant countries in this period).

If you need to learn more about working with regnal years, saint's days, and these other dating practices, C. R. Cheney's *A Handbook of Dates* is the key source of information.

Imprint Statements

An imprint statement consists of information about who printed the book, where it was printed, and when. Most hand-press books include that information on the bottom of the title page, but incunabula often use a colophon at the end of a book instead. (For more on the general development of the title page, see "Title Pages" in this part.)

The use of colophons comes from the manuscript tradition, in which scribes often concluded a text with information about who wrote it and where and when it was made. In early printed books, which tended to follow the same textual habits as manuscripts, imprint information was shared in colophons at the end of a text. Although not as immediately decipherable as the imprint formulations that developed later, colophons usually named the printer, date, and location of printing.

As the title page developed, such imprint information moved to the bottom of the title page. There it often followed a standard formula, naming the location, then the personnel involved, and the year it was printed. Not all of the information provided, however, is as clear-cut as it can appear to be.

Locations were typically cities given by their vernacular or Latin names. For example, Venice might be identified as Venetiis, or Liège as Leodij. (There are resources that can help identify Latin place names; see "Catalog and Imprint Resources" in Appendix 1.) Locations might also be falsified in the case of works that might antagonize authorities or that were pirated. Sometimes the false imprint is obvious: Thomas Scott's argument against the marriage of an English prince to a Spanish princess, *Robert Earle of Essex his ghost, sent from Elizian.: to the nobility, gentry, and communaltie of England* (STC 22084), identifies itself as having been "Printed in Paradise" although it was printed in London. Other false imprints can be harder for the novice to identify: the first (unauthorized) edition of the collected poems of John Wilmot, Earl of Rochester, (Wing R1753) has an imprint location of Antwerp, but was probably printed in London (as suggested by the appearance of the signatures and catchwords).

Information about the various roles of printers, publishers, and booksellers can also be provided in the imprint statement, although the vocabulary used might not correspond with ours today. (Remember that the early modern book trade didn't differentiate "publisher" as a separate category.) A common formulation in English books is "was printed by XY for AB" in which we can understand XY as the printer and AB as the publisher. Sometimes, however, a statement might leave out the printer: "printed for AB." More confusing is the formulation "printed by AB" in which "printed by" should be understood as "caused to be printed"—that is, AB was responsible for getting the book printed, but was not the person who did the actual printing. Often catalog records will help clarify what role people acted in if it's not clear from the statement. (See "Catalog Records" in Part 5 for more information on working with catalogs.) Sometimes different imprints will be on different versions of a book. If a group of sellers published a book together, there might be a separate title page for each of them with their individual information (see "Edition, Impression, Issue, State, Copy" later in this part for an example of this practice).

English book imprints often include information about where a book is to be sold, as in this edition of Elizabeth Jocelin's *The mothers legacie, to her unborne childe*: "London: Printed by F. K. for Robert Allot, and are to be sold in Pauls Church-yard, at the signe of the Blacke Beare, 1635" (STC 14625.7). This identifies where a book is available for wholesale to other members of the Stationers' Company (the guild that controlled the London book trade). But the book was also available for sale to the public by other booksellers.

The final piece of imprint information provided is the date. This is usually straightforward, but not always. Just as other aspects of the imprint statement may be falsified to cover up illegitimate printing, so too may the date be altered. (Unauthorized or illegitimate printing happened for many reasons, including piracy and censorship; printing under a false imprint provided some cover from punishment.) The date may also have been altered to reflect when it was anticipated that the book would be sold rather than when it was printed; if a book was printed late in the calendar year, the imprint date might be the next year. (For more, see "Dates" earlier in this part.)

Edition, Impression, Issue, State, Copy

The text of hand-press books could exist in different versions, whether due to silent changes to correct errors or deliberate changes to differentiate between different versions. The vocabulary used to describe these different versions is helpful in understanding what you're working with.

An edition of a book encompasses all copies of a book made from (mostly) the same setting of type. Some books exist in multiple editions—printed at a later date, for example, or in a different location—but many were only printed in a single edition. If a substantial number of changes have been made to the text, then it is a new edition; generally speaking, the rule of thumb is whether more than half of the text has been reset.

If only some of the type has been reset (that is, if it's part of a single edition), then a single copy of the book might belong to one of the subsets of impression, issue, and state. An impression is the set of copies of an edition that were printed at any one time. In the hand-press period, since type was usually distributed after each forme was done being printed, impression and edition tend to mean the same thing (but do not always).

An issue is the set of copies of an impression that vary from the idealized version of an edition in a specific way planned by the publisher. An example of an issue might be a different title page: the 1577 edition of *Holinshed's Chronicles* (STC 13568), for example, was printed by a group of stationers, each of whom had an issue of that edition with their name featured as the printer. Other examples of issues might be the printing of the book on large paper (that is, larger sheets that provided wider margins). In general, issues are usually meant by the publisher to be identified as a deliberate and distinct group.

A state refers to all other variants; it can be helpful to think of states as consisting of those changes that the printer or publisher might not wish to call attention to. The inclusion of stop-press changes are usually described in terms of a corrected (as opposed to an uncorrected) state of that edition. The insertion of cancels and the addition of extra text are also examples of different states of an edition. When talking about stop-press changes in particular, it's necessary to remember that not all sheets in a copy might include all such changes; the sheet that makes up the B gathering might have stop-press changes, and thereby be described as being in the corrected state, while the D gathering might be in its uncorrected state.

Finally, a copy is a single instance of a book and it is always unique. It's what you hold in your hand. A copy might differ from what is described in articles about a work or in a catalog record. Both of those tend to work from ideal copies—that version of an edition that is imagined as perfect, with all the corrections and later changes incorporated into a single ideal. An ideal copy might not, in fact, exist. If there are two surviving copies of a book, with copy 1 consisting of signatures A and B and copy 2 consisting of signatures B and C, the ideal copy of the book would be one that included signatures A, B, and C. The first quarto of *Hamlet* (STC 22275) is a good example of this. There are only two extant (that is, surviving) copies, one of which has the title page but not the final leaf, the other of which has the final leaf but not the title page; the collation statement of the ideal copy (4°: $[A]^2$ (–A1) B–I^4) assumes both leaves are present.

This vocabulary of edition, impression, issue, and state is largely a modern one. Printers in the hand-press period often used such terms differently. Edition and impression, for example, could be used interchangeably, with a title page describing a book as a "second impression" rather than a "second edition." When in doubt, catalogers have often standardized the description in their records. But it also worth noting that catalogs aren't always precise about this, especially the older projects; the STC, for example, sometimes describes (and numbers) different states as different editions. (See more about the STC and other catalogs in Appendix 1, "Catalogs of Early Hand-press Books.")

Initial Letters

Initial letters are the decorated letters that you see at the beginning of a section of text. The practice of decorating initials comes from the manuscript tradition, which relied on decorated initials in part to visually signal the start of a new section at a time when texts were generally large black blocks of words without visual breaks.

In incunables, blank spaces were often left for decorated initials to be added by hand later. Sometimes in those blank spaces guide letters were included—printed letters that showed the scribe what letter was to be drawn there. Not all blank spaces were filled with decorated letters. Sometimes an owner would choose to leave those spaces blank; sometimes a later owner would crudely supply their own initials. To our eyes, these blank spaces can make a book look unfinished, although clearly they didn't bother all earlier users.

As printing evolved, initial letters became part of the printing process, with woodblock illustrations used instead of hand-drawn letters. These woodblocks could depict letters surrounded by abstract decorations, or they could include pictures of plants, animals, cherubs, or other figures. Some initials, known as factotum, consisted of

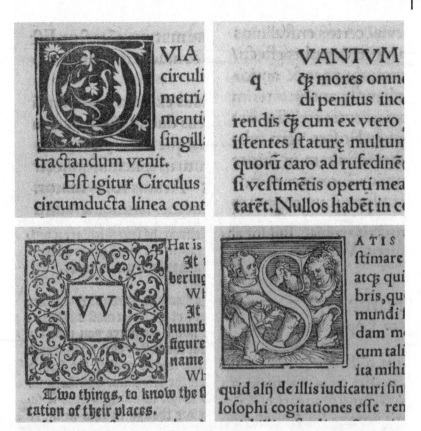

Figure 33 Examples of different forms of initial letters. On the top row are two "q"s: a decorated initial and a guide letter, both from Waldseemüller's 1507 *Cosmographiae introduction* (USTC 206973). On the bottom left is a factotum of the letter "w" (here depicted with two "v"s) from Blundeville's 1613 *Exercises* (STC 3149). Bottom right is an historiated "s" from Copernicus's 1543 *De revolvtionibvs orbium cœlestium* (VD16 K 2099). From public domain images made available by the Library of Congress (top row: E125.V6W15, sigs. A3r, b6v; bottom left: QB41 .B598, sig. B1r; bottom right: QB41 .C76 1543, sig. iiv).

borders around a space into which a piece of type could be placed. Generally these initial letters are not tied specifically to the text as illustrations of it. These woodblocks, like other decorative woodblocks, are used over and over in different texts. But sometimes an initial letter will be designed specifically to connect to the text—a bible might have initial letters at the start of a book that connect to its text. But those are rare exceptions to the general practice of printers using initials based on whether they fit the space.

Marginal Notes

Although we tend to use the word "marginalia" to refer to handwritten comments in books, the term more properly refers to any notes in the margin of a book, including those that are printed. Texts today include references and comments as footnotes at the bottom

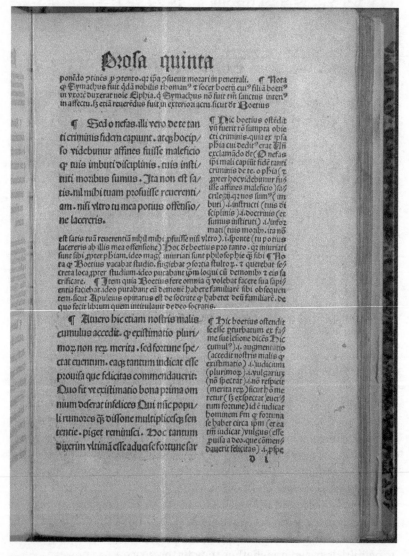

Figure 34 In this 1497 edition of Boethius's *De consolatione philosophiae* (GW 04563), the main text (the blocks of large font) are surrounded by commentary (the smaller type). Public domain image made available by Universitäts- und Stadtbibliothek Köln (sig. d1r).

of a page or as endnotes at the back of the book or chapter. But in the early centuries of printing, reference notes, glosses, and commentary were often printed in the margins.

We also tend to think of marginalia as marginal—that is, as something that is unimportant or not central to the work. But early printed books also used margins to print commentary that was, in fact, the point of the book. Commentary on classical and religious works drew on a mise-en-page established in the manuscript tradition of placing a small amount of text on a page and surrounding it with notes.

Marginal notes were printed at the same time as the rest of the book. They would be set on the composing stick separately (and usually in a smaller font) and then locked into the chase in their proper location.

While their content can be useful, so can thinking about what their presence signals about the intended audience of the book. Bibles after the Reformation were often printed with marginal notes pointing to connections across the books, often between the gospels or linking the Old Testament and the New Testament; those notes suggest a way of reading the text different from the unadorned bibles of earlier periods.

Music

Because music required notes printed on top of staves (the lines on which notes are positioned), it was not as straightforward to print as text. In the incunabula period, initially only the staves were printed, with the notes added in by hand later. By the 1470s, the innovation was developed of running music through the press twice: first to print the staves, and then to print the notes. The trick with that technique is that not only is it time-consuming, it's difficult to get the two printings to register precisely—if the alignment is off just a little bit, the wrong note would be played. In the 16th century, printers switched to using single pieces of type that combined short lines of staff with the note itself. A series of musical notes could be printed in one pass by combining the different pieces of type with the correct length of notes in the right places on the staff. The end result was legible, and accurate, albeit not especially tidy, as the staves were broken up into what look like dashes rather than solid lines. Eventually music printing came to be dominated by engraved plates in which finer precision and continuous lines made the music more accurate and easier to read.

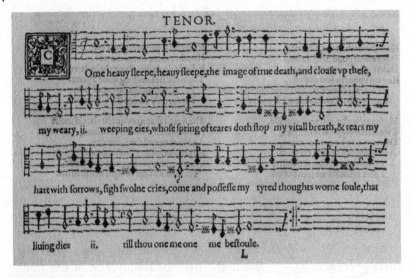

Figure 35 The alto part to John Dowland's song "Come, heavy sleepe" in the 1597 *The First Booke of Songes* (STC 7091). Each individual note is printed, along with the staff, with a separate piece of type. From a public domain image made available by the Boston Public Library (RARE BKS G.400.51 FOLIO, sig. L1r).

Pagination and Foliation

The practice of numbering a book's pages developed over the hand-press period. Initially books followed manuscript practice of numbering leaves, a practice we call foliation ("folio" here refers to leaves, not to format). During the 16th century, pagination was introduced, and by the 17th century it was more common to see pages numbered than leaves. Errors in pagination are not unusual, especially in the early years of their usage. And page numbers can repeat from one section of a book to the next, so referring to "page 52" in a book that has multiple paginated sections isn't helpful. For both of these reasons, it's often preferable to use signature marks as your point of reference.

Preliminary Leaves

The parts of a text that come at the front of the book—title page, dedications, letters to the reader—are referred to as the book's preliminary leaves or prelims. Although prelims come first when you read the book, they are typically printed last, after the main text has been completed. Often preliminary materials were the last to be written— commendatory texts might still be in the process of being gathered, for example, or dedications being created—and printing this section last was practical. And since the nature of prelims is to be separate from and introductory to the main body of text, printing them out of sequence didn't affect the rest of the book.

One consequence is that the preliminary leaves might be signed differently than the rest of the book, with symbols instead of letters, for instance. (See "Signature Marks" in in this part for more information.) Another is that prelims were sometimes printed in a different imposition than the rest of the book, or printed on the same sheet as the final gathering. The last gathering in an octavo, for example, might consist of four leaves signed G that were printed along with four leaves of preliminary materials signed A. By combining the two gatherings on a single sheet, the printer is able to use a full sheet rather than two partial sheets.

Press Figures

In the late 17th and 18th centuries, British and American printers often kept track of their work by using small numbers, letters, or other symbols to identify which pages they had set. These figures are typically placed at the bottom of a page in the direction line, often on the verso to separate them from signature marks. Individual figures were linked to specific printers and could be tracked to see how much work that printer had done and what wages they were owed. Differing accounts suggest the practice wasn't standardized; pressmen could have been paid by how much they set (in which case, you'd expect to see press figures on every forme) or by how long they worked (which wouldn't seem to be tracked by individual formes).

Even without understanding the full details of how they were assigned, the bibliographer can use press figures to help differentiate between different impressions of an edition. William Todd, in his foundational study, demonstrates how changes in figures or in their position can indicate a disruption in the book's printing. And because press figures occur primarily in books printed in Britain and (formerly) British colonies, book historians have sometimes used the presence of press figures in a continental book to argue that it's a false imprint. But as Robert Dawson demonstrates, press figures were occasionally used in France and cannot be automatically assumed to be a false imprint.

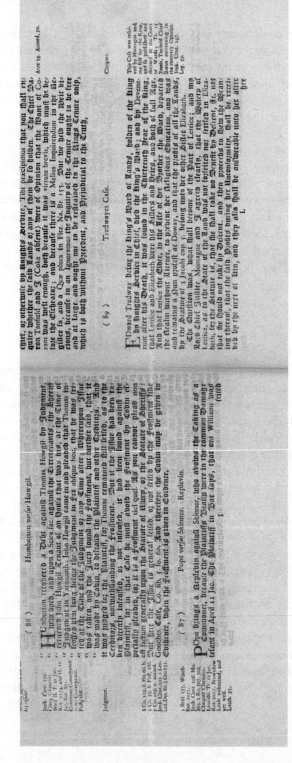

Figure 36 The press figure 3 can be seen on the bottom of the left-hand side of the opening in the direction line along with the catchword "seised." On the right-hand side of the direction line is the signature mark "L" and the catchword "her." This detail comes from the 1724 collected reports of Henry Hobart, the Chief Justice of the Court of Common Pleas in England from 1613 to 1625 (ESTC T112687). You can also see the use of marginal notes referring to other cases and the use of blackletter for the main text, a common characteristic of English legal texts. Public domain image made available by the Boston Public Library (RARE BKS Adams 82.3 Folio, sigs K4v–L1r).

Printer's Devices

On many title pages in the hand-press period are small pictures below the title and above the imprint statement. These are not illustrations, but printer's devices—images that identify the printer or publisher of the book. (They can also sometimes be found at the back of a book.) They are akin to, and the forerunners of, the small logos you see on many of today's printed books, like the small penguin on Penguin imprints or the seagull on Norton books.

Such devices were usually related in some fashion to the printer himself. Devices in the first years of printing might represent the sign of the shop. (In the early modern period, there weren't numbered street addresses the way locations are identified today, but visually identifiable signs; many pubs still harken back to this tradition with their names and signs.) More common were devices that punned on or were rebuses for a printer's name; Thomas Fisher, for example, used a kingfisher. Other printers used emblems. Perhaps the most well-known in this category is the dolphin wrapped around an anchor used as Aldine press's device, an emblem for "make haste slowly," a caution to be both productive and careful that is a good motto for a press.

Although some printers changed their devices over the course of their careers, devices were often consistent enough that they can be used to identify a printer even when he is not named. Book historians have used devices to identify printers in this manner as well as to recognize pirated editions, which often used a device that didn't correspond to the imprint information. Catalogs of printer's devices can be found in Appendix 1. (It's good to remember, though, that not all images that appear on a title page are devices. Sometimes there will be a coat of arms or emblem belonging to the author or a book's patron, or an illustration related to the content of the book itself.)

Printer's Ornaments

Printers typically kept a stock of type to use as design elements. These could consist of small metal-cast pieces of type known as printer's flowers or fleurons, although not all such pieces were of flowers; these pieces of type could be used individually, but more typically were combined to form larger designs. They could also consist of larger woodcut pieces, such as borders, headpieces, or tailpieces, that served to decorate and to set off the beginning and ending of sections of a book. Ornaments were not typically used as illustrations that connected with a book's text, but as page fillers (including as a sort of inked bearing type) or methods of demarcating the beginnings and ends of a text. They were often shared among printers, and so are not a reliable indicator on their own of a printer's identity.

Privileges, Approbations, and Imprimaturs

Different systems of authority and permission affected the ability to publish something, with those systems changing across location and time. But there are some common features across the hand-press period that might leave their marks on the page.

One of the most frequent marks you'll see is an indication that a book was published by "privilege"—that is, an institution of authority (a monarch, government, or guild, typically) would grant a printer the right to print a book or category of books for a set period of time. This right was often exclusive and assigned to books that were guaranteed sellers, such as bibles or law books. The right to print these books was sometimes signaled by a statement at the end of the book, on the title page ("cum privilegio"), or on its own page immediately following the title page. After the rise of authorial copyright, the system of assigning privileges to printers faded.

Permission from an authority was often required before publication. In some places this authority might be a government, in other places a church, or some combination of the two. Typically the text would be shown to the required authority before printing; if approved by the authority, printing could proceed. The final imprimaturs were sometimes required to be printed on the book, and can be found in the book's front matter in the form of an approbation statement or a *nihil obstat* (nothing objected) as evidence from an earlier approval from the church.

Signature Marks

Signature marks indicate the order of sheets and their leaves. If a book is to be made up of eight sheets in a quarto imposition, then each sheet is marked to indicate its place in the order so they are assembled in the correct order. The most frequently used indication of order is the 23-letter Latin alphabet (A to Z, omitting either I or J, either U or V, and W; see "Alphabet" in this part for more detail). If it is a long book, the series might have to be run through multiple times, with A–Z followed by AA–ZZ, AAA–ZZZ, etc. (In the 18th century, English printers often represented such signatures as 2A, 3A, etc., a practice that is usually used by bibliographers today.) Because the preliminaries of a book were usually printed last, they were often signed differently. If the main text began with a gathering signed "A," then the preliminaries might be signed "a" or with symbols like "*" or "¶."

Not only did the sheets need to be gathered in the correct order, they needed to folded so that the leaves were in the correct sequence. And so in addition to indicating the gathering order, signature marks also indicate the sequence of leaves with either arabic or roman numerals. For our hypothetical quarto, you'll need to know, at a minimum, which are the first and second leaves so that you can fold the sheet correctly; for an octavo, you'll need to know the first, second, third, and fourth leaves. (In both, once you have the first half of the leaves in the correct order, the remaining leaves fall into place.)

We tend, today, to use signature marks primarily as page numbers— a way of identifying what page or leaf we are looking at. If, for instance, I was working with an English book in which a poem appeared on the fourth page of the main text, I would identify that as "sig. B2v": it's in the "B" gathering on the second leaf on the verso side. (The two sides of a leaf are described as its "recto" and its "verso"— the front and back.) Even if a leaf isn't signed (that is, printed with a signature mark) you can still identify it this way—just count forward from the last printed signature and you'll work out which leaf it is.

While we focus on signature marks as a method of location within a book, they can also identify where a work was printed. Although signature marks all follow the same basic formula of identifying gathering and leaf, within that basic structure are variations. Are leaf numbers indicated with roman or arabic numerals? Are the preliminaries signed with letters of the alphabet or with symbols? Is the first half of the gathering's leaves signed or the first half plus one?

In 1966, R. A. Sayce published the results of his examination of over 2,800 books printed in 10 different countries, an effort to determine whether compositors followed local practices in signing books printed between 1530 and 1800. His study showed that there are variations in signature marks, catchwords, pagination, press figures, and imprint dates tied to geographical regions. For instance, English books typically start signing the main text with B, saving A for the preliminary materials; books printed in Antwerp frequently sign preliminaries with * but books from Paris rarely do; and if you're looking at a book using ¶ in the preliminaries, it's likely to have been printed in Geneva. For books that are printed anonymously, or that try to surreptitiously pass themselves off as having been printed elsewhere, such clues can help bibliographers locate a book's origins.

Title Pages

We take title pages for granted: at the front of a book, there's a page that states the title and author of the work, along with the publisher and sometimes the date it was published. But the existence and format of title pages is something that has evolved as the conditions of printing have changed. When you look at a hand-press book, you might find an elaborate, illustrated title page. Or you might see a plain title page with a long, descriptive title, or perhaps a plain page with only a brief title shown. Maybe you'll not see a title page at all, and the book will immediately begin with the text itself. The best overview of the development of the early title page is Margaret Smith's *The Title-page: Its Early Development, 1460–1510*, which provides an argument based on the material conditions of publishing and plenty of examples of what early title pages looked like. The overview here draws heavily on her research. (For more on understanding who printed a book and related publication information, see the sections in this part on dates, imprint statements, and printer's devices.)

Medieval manuscripts generally did not have title pages. The first page of those codices instead begin immediately with the text of the work, sometimes preceded by the Latin word "incipit" ("here begins") and a short title for the work. But as printing presses allowed for mass production of books, the need both to protect books from damage while in storage and to advertise books for sale led to gradual changes in how books were identified.

The first shift was moving the start of the text from the first page to the second or third page. Smith argues that the shift to mass production of books meant that there were inevitably books that had to be stored for perhaps long periods of time, and thus it was important to protect the first page of text from getting damaged. Since books were typically stored folded lengthwise in quires before being bound, moving the text from the first page to the second or the third shifts it from the outside to an inside, protected position.

Once the text had moved to an inside position, however, another problem arose. If you have stacks of books waiting to be moved from warehouse to bookshop, how do you know which blank gatherings are which books? The obvious answer was to put label-titles on the first page of the book, brief titles that served to quickly identify what the text was.

With the shift to having to sell books that, at first glance, were not readily identifiable beyond a brief phrase came the need to market books. Titles become longer, authors were often named, and (due in part to growing regulation over the printing industry) imprint information was added. Decoration might be included, sometimes as woodcut borders or illustrations, sometimes as full-page, detailed engravings; of course, more elaborate title pages often needed to be protected, and so blank front leaves were reintroduced. In other words, the title page shifted from being merely informative to being a marketing tool. Indeed, title pages were often displayed on their own as advertisements. These conventions, established by the early 16th century, held through the hand-press period.

One of the tricky things about working with this range of title-page styles, however, is determining how to identify the title of a book. If you encounter a book that was printed without a title page, the title is usually taken from the incipit or the opening lines of text. In some cases, as in the famous work printed by William Caxton in 1477, this can be initially confusing: *Whan that Apprill with his shouris sote* (the transcription of the opening line of the poem) is more commonly known as *Canterbury Tales* (STC 5082).

In other cases, you might encounter the opposite problem: the title of the work is nearly as long as the work itself. The play we refer to as *King Lear* was first published as a quarto in 1608 with the title *M. William Shak-speare: his true chronicle historie of the life and death of King Lear and his three daughters.: With the vnfortunate life of Edgar, sonne and heire to the Earle of Gloster, and his sullen and assumed humor of Tom of Bedlam: as it was played before the Kings Maiestie at Whitehall vpon S. Stephans night in Christmas hollidayes. By his Maiesties seruants playing vsually at the Gloabe on the Bancke-side* (STC 22292). There are usually accepted short titles for such works that should be used instead of the ones on the title page. It's helpful, in these cases, to also look at the "uniform title" field in catalog records to identify what the book is; it is often acceptable to refer to such works by their uniform title. (See "Catalog Records" in Part 5 for more tips on navigating catalogs.)

Volvelles and Movable Figures

Volvelles are movable diagrams made from disks or other shapes of paper layered on top of each other and pinned in the middle so that they can each turn separately. (The name comes from the Latin *volvere*, "to turn.") By lining up different pieces of information on the various layers of the volvelle, a user could make a range of calculations.

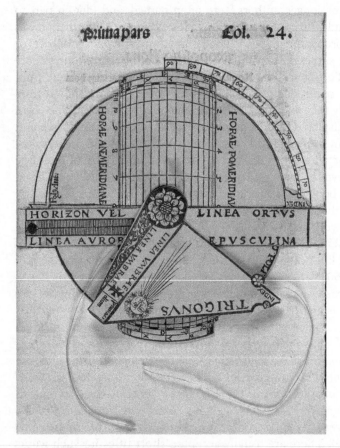

Figure 37 This four-part movable diagram is from the 1524 first edition of Peter Apian's *Cosmographicus libre* (VD16 A 3080). With this volvelle, the user can practice a series of complicated calculations, including latitude, the times of sunrise and sunset, the duration of dawn and dusk, and the height of the sun. Apian used his volvelle as a way of proving to his reader the accuracy of his propositions; it wasn't merely a decorative add-on, but an integral part of the text. Public domain image made available by the Smithsonian Libraries (GA6.A4X, sig. C4v).

They were popular tools for astronomy and navigation books, but were also used for making and breaking ciphers and for divination.

Volvelles were printed as separate discs, with the bottom layer printed as part of the forme along with the text. The top layers were printed on separate sheets, so that they could be cut out and sewn onto the appropriate page either during the binding process or by the owner. While volvelles were clearly intended to be assembled to work, it's not unusual to see copies of books missing the movable layers, and sometimes you find those layers bound in as sheets in the back of the book. The uncut parts are sometimes printed on what appears to be scrap paper, rather than regularly shaped leaves or sheets, suggesting the reuse of waste paper. Anthony Drennan's work on volvelles reveals the range of ways in which they were constructed; Suzanne Kerr looks at the range of uses and meanings associated with movable parts.

Other types of movable diagrams are found in hand-press books as well. Flaps that you can lift were popular and useful in anatomy books, allowing a user to see different layers of a body—the inside of a uterus, for example, or the muscles under the skin. Less spectacular, but equally fragile, are fold-out charts and diagrams that extend the size of a page.

Part 4

Looking at Books

Now that we've learned something about how early printed books were made and what they look like, it's time to put this toolbox in service to working with such books. The first step in this process is to look at a book. We're all used to reading a book, but looking at a book—noting all of its physical features—is not usually something that we've been trained to do. For most purposes, we are interested in what a book says and so we focus on its text. But a book also says things through its physical expression, such as how the text is laid out on the page (its mise-en-page), what typefaces are used, how it's bound, and what the paper is like that it's printed on. These factors, whether we are aware of them or not, shape how we read and respond to the book. And in hand-press books, looking at the physical aspects of a book can help us not only guess at some of the intentions of the publisher and the reception by users, but also find details that reveal how the book was made.

In this part of our guide, I focus on what should be the first step when meeting a hand-press book: looking at it. My assumption is that you are looking at a physical copy of a book, but much of what I advise can and should also be done with digital images of

---

How books mean through their physical expression

This guide focuses primarily on how books were made, with some suggestions about how to interpret aspects of their making. (Those "Why does it Matter?" sections in Part 2 offer evidence of such approaches.) Using bibliographic tools to understand how a book makes meaning is a next important step. In his foundational *Bibliography and the Sociology of Texts*, D. F. McKenzie argues for an approach to bibliography that is not happy merely to understand how books were made, but that strives to understand how books mean both as objects and as texts. In other words, we must look at a book in order to know how to read it. McKenzie's work, and other recommended readings in Appendix 1, will help you explore how books make meaning through their physical expression.

Studying Early Printed Books 1450–1800: A Practical Guide, First Edition. Sarah Werner.
© 2019 Sarah Werner. Published 2019 by John Wiley & Sons Ltd.

hand-press books; the last section focuses explicitly on working with digital facsimiles. In Part 5, "Afterlives of Books," I will discuss how to identify what parts of a book might have been changed after it was made (new bindings, for instance, or repaired leaves). But here the important thing is to note details without worrying about their time frame.

My general approach to looking at books is to work from the outside in: the first thing you notice about a book is how big it is and what its binding looks like. From there you move to noticing the contents of the book, such as whether there's a title page, what typefaces are used, and if there are illustrations. Finally, you notice how the book has survived the centuries, looking for signs of wear or of readers' uses of it.

The hardest part of looking at a book is not reading it. If you start reading the book before you look at it, it is too easy to get absorbed in the text and to miss its physical characteristics. One of the best ways to learn how to look at a book is to work with one you can't read. If you can find a book that's in a language you don't know—or, even better, in an alphabet you don't know—that's a great way to practice these skills. And you'll be surprised by how much you can learn about a book you can't read!

Since the process of looking at books is really one best approached as a step-by-step list of questions to ask, what follows is written as an outline of questions to prompt your examination, with some asides about what you might learn from what you see.

Good Research Habits

Before you start looking at books, or even finding books to look at, it's good to take a moment to establish how you're going to organize your research. There are some basic good habits for note-taking that will save you frustrations down the line:

- Record the shelfmark or call number of the book you're examining; if you're working in multiple libraries, be sure to include that information as well.
- Record the basic information of the book: author, short title, date of publication.
- Clearly differentiate notes on different books; starting a new file or a new piece of paper with each book can keep notes from getting mixed up.

- Record the signature mark for every observation or note you write down; remember, pagination is often not as reliable as signature marks.
- If you are taking notes by hand, be sure to differentiate your abbreviations for recto and verso; many of us have handwriting that makes it hard to tell "r" and "v" apart.
- Decide whether or not you're going to quote from the work as semi-diplomatic transcriptions or if you're going to modernize; there are benefits and drawbacks to each, but I prefer to do semi-diplomatic transcriptions in case I make any modernization errors and can't go back to check the source.
- If you are taking notes on your computer, turn off spelling corrections; early modern spelling is different and if your word processing program changes "deere" to "deer" instead of "dear," your notes won't be accurate.
- If you're using a computer, think about how you're going to name your files; three different files called "1631 almanac" won't be useful but "1631_almanac_green_binding" could do a better job of jogging your memory.
- If you are taking photos, plan how you're going to organize them. Your camera will assign file names to them, but it's more helpful to rename them with shelfmarks or titles so you can easily identify them later.

Handling Books

Before you can look at a book, you'll need to learn how to handle rare materials properly. Every library will have its own procedures and rules to ensure the safety of its collections. But there are some general principles that will always be applicable.

The first thing to know is what you can and cannot bring into a reading room when you're working with rare books. The basic rule is that anything that could permanently alter a book should be left behind—no pens, highlighters, food, drink, gum, cough drops, scissors, or glue, for example. Some libraries will ask you to only bring in a notebook and pencils, others will allow you to bring in small bags, laptops, and cameras (although always keep your flash turned off!). It's best to check before your first visit what the procedures are.

The next step, before you retrieve any materials, should be to wash your hands. Lotions, moisturizers, the general gunk that accumulates over the course of a day—these can leave behind damaging oils when you touch a book. So not only should you have clean, lotion-free hands when you enter a reading room, you should wash your hands periodically while you're doing your research, especially after handling any volumes bound in leather that might be flaking.

Once you have an item at your desk, your goal is similarly to avoid doing anything that might damage it. Don't lean over your book with your pencil in hand, since that might accidentally mark it. Avoid running your fingers along the printed text or manuscript marks. Turn pages slowly, avoiding fragile corners or edges.

Avoiding damage to rare materials also means supporting them adequately. Book supports are usually foam or beanbag pieces that can be arranged so that when you rest the book on them, it is cradled safely. Bindings generally do not want to be opened more than 120°; tight ones often shouldn't be opened past 90°. If you open a book slowly and feel for resistance, you'll quickly sense where the binding stops. That's how the book should rest in its cradle. Libraries also provide book weights to use to hold your book open, and you should use those weights rather than holding it open with your hands. As you make your way through the book, you will need to rearrange its position on the cradle so that it remains supported.

Sometimes you'll get a book that comes in a box, a plastic sleeve, or that is wrapped in ties. These are usually an indication that the book is in need of conservation treatment and should be handled with extra care. The most common problem you'll encounter is a detached board, where one or both of the boards have come off the book entirely. If that's the case, it's usually best to place the board aside and put the text block on the cradle.

If you're working with unbound material, leave it flat on the desk while reading it, rather than holding it in your hands. If it's

A note about book smells

Go ahead and smell your book! Sometimes people make jokes about how digital books don't have that real book smell, or they comment about the fusty smell of old libraries. But while those comments can be dismissive, it is true that books have a smell, and sometimes that smell can convey useful information about a book. A book's smell can indicate the presence of mold and the need for conservation. It could smell of a former owner's pipe smoking. Or it could simply smell like the normal aging of rag paper and leather bindings. (See, for instance, the work of Strlič et al. on chemical analysis of old paper.)

But where are the gloves?

Popular culture tends to show people wearing white cotton gloves when handling rare books, but a recent study has shown that wearing gloves can cause more damage than clean hands (see Baker and Silverman). Gloves make it hard to feel what you're touching, thus increasing the odds of accidentally tearing a leaf. And gloves are often not regularly washed, thereby creating the risk that dirt and oils could be transferred from one book to another. Some libraries do still require the use of gloves (and gloves are usually necessary for handling materials like photographs, metals, and textiles), so always follow the rules of your library.

in a folder as part of a series of documents, leave them in the order you find them.

In general, use common sense and always ask a librarian for assistance if you're not sure how to handle something or if you notice damage. A number of libraries have produced videos that demonstrate good handling practices; the Folger Shakespeare Library's does a nice job of showing different materials and cases (see the link in Appendix 1).

Appearance

What is this?

- *Is this a book? A pamphlet? A fragment?*
  How would you describe the object in front of you? What characteristics jump out at you? Is it difficult or easy to categorize?

Size

- *Approximately how big is your book?*
  You don't need a ruler for this; try thinking along the lines of "about as tall as my hand" or "about the size of a regular piece of paper" or "wow this thing is heavy!" The size of your book can help you think about its intended uses; a large book cannot be carried around, and a small book is unlikely to have been read from at a lectern.
- *How many pages are in your book?*
  You can think of this in terms of page count or in terms of "depth" of the book if it's not paginated or foliated.

Binding

- *Is your item bound? What does the binding look like?*
  Observe its color, texture, and the presence or absence of decoration. If you know what it's made of, that should be noted, even if it's

no more specific than "some kind of leather." These and the following aspects of bindings can suggest how a book is intended to be used and how much it is (or is not) valued.

- *Is the book housed in a box or another sort of case?*
  If it is, is that a signal that the binding is fragile or precious? Does the box seem to be made for protection or for display?
- *Are the fore-edges of the book gilt or otherwise decorated?*
  The edges of a book can range from plain to fancy to very fancy. In addition to being gilt, they might be gauffered (have designs cut into the paper) or sometimes painted with pictures that only reveal themselves when the leaves are fanned. You might also find titles inscribed on the edges of books, or there might not be any markings or decoration at all.
- *What do the pastedowns and endleaves look like?*
  Are they made from decorative papers or paper otherwise notably different from the text block? Sometimes waste paper (discarded manuscripts or printed texts) are reused in the binding, either as pastedowns or visible underneath loose pastedowns.

Paper

- *What color is the paper in the text block?*
  For example, you might see colors you'd describe as "light cream" or "yellowed" or even "blue" or "pink." Are there leaves or sections of the volume in which the paper is noticeably different? Changes in paper stock can indicate that those leaves come from a different copy. They can also be due to pages being exposed to light while on display or to other effects of damage. Such evidence can help us understand the book's history.
- *What texture is the paper?*
  Paper can feel thick or thin, flat or warped, stiff or flexible; you can get a sense of how it feels simply from turning the leaves or by running your finger over the margins, avoiding any printed text or manuscript marginalia so that you don't accidentally damage the book. The texture of the paper can be affected by how it was originally made or by later treatments by collectors and booksellers.
- *Are there chain lines?*
  You should look at multiple leaves in the book, at least, if not the entire volume. Noting the presence and direction of chain lines is necessary for identifying the format of the book. Variations in the

chain lines can help you identify leaves that aren't original to the book or that suggest some hiccup in its printing. Exclude the end-leaves in your examination, since those are part of the binding and will differ from the text block.

- *Are there watermarks?*
  This can be time-consuming, but it can also be helpful at this stage to work through at least a few gatherings to see on which leaves and in what position marks can be found. At some point you might need to go through all the leaves in the book, noting not only the location of watermarks but their appearance and whether there are multiple marks. Again, exclude the endleaves from this examination.

Contents

Title Page

- *Is there a title page?*
  Not all books have a title page; it might have been an early book printed without one, or it might have had one that has been subsequently lost. (The first and last leaves of a book are particularly susceptible to damage since they are more exposed and more frequently handled than the rest of the text block.) Some books have title pages for different sections of the book; if that is the case, note those, but at this point in the exercise, concentrate on the one that is relevant to the whole work.
- *What sort of information does it seem to provide?*
  Typical features include some or all of the following: title of the work, author, printer, publisher, location, and date. There might also be descriptive text providing information about the nature or history of the work or of the author, an epigraph, persons named other than the author, or other text or images. How does such information market the book? What features does it call attention to?
- *What does it look like?*
  Title pages can range from the plain to the highly decorated. Are there borders or rules surrounding the page? Is there a printer's device? Is it illustrated? What typefaces are used? Is there a frontispiece facing it? Does its appearance suggest any intended audiences for the book? How does the title page work as an advertisement for the book?

Colophon

- *Is there a colophon?*
  Colophons are primarily a feature of incunabula, so the majority of early printed books won't have them. Especially if your book does not have a title page, or has a title page that does not provide imprint information, be sure to look for a colophon at the end of the work. (Occasionally a colophon will be found in the preliminary material.)
- *What sort of information does it seem to provide?*
  Typical features include some or all of the following: title, printer's name, location, and date. They sometimes include additional information, like praise for the work or thanks for its completion.

Navigation

- *Does your book use page numbers?*
  Page numbers are a later development in printed books, and many do not have them. If yours does, do they seem to be correct? Are they divided into separate sequences?
- *Is it foliated?*
  Early books are more likely to be foliated instead of paginated; that is, they count leaves rather than pages. If yours is foliated, does the order seem to be correct? Is the numbering divided into separate sequences?
- *Are there other text divisions to assist in navigation?*
  Examples of other types of textual divisions are chapters, acts and scenes, and sectional breaks into parts or books. Being aware of textual divisions can help you think about how the book was designed to be used.
- *Is there an index?*
  We are used to non-fiction works having an index at the end of the book to help readers jump to specific topics. But the development of indices, like that of other print conventions, was a process. You might look for an index at the back of a book. If there is one, how is it organized? What sort of categories does it use? Different organizational schemes can offer a clue as to how the book's makers and users thought of it.
- *Is there a table of contents?*
  We would expect a modern book to have a table of contents at the front of the book, just after the title page. But not all early

printed books used tables of contents. If your book has one, where is it? What sort of sections is it divided into? Is it displayed as a list, or perhaps as a graphic chart? What does it suggest about how the book should be used?

Categories of Text

- *Do there seem to be different categories of text in your book?*
  All books will have some sort of main text that is their primary content. But many will have additional categories of text, such as a preface, letters to the reader, or dedications. The presence of such parts can help you imagine the intended audience and use of the book.
- *Are there printed marginal notes?*
  Texts might have notes printed in the margins to act as navigational aids ("this is where the history of Boadicea starts"), as references ("this is the source for this information") and cross-references (particularly in Bibles, there might be indications of other places in the text that discuss the same topic), and as commentary. The presence of marginal notes can be a sign of how the book was intended to be used. What uses are suggested by the notes in your book?
- *Is there an errata list?*
  Some books include a list of errors made in its printing. This errata list might appear at the end of the volume or at the end of the preliminaries. Does anything jump out at you about the errors? Are they clustered in one part of the book? Are they mostly spelling errors or more substantive mistakes?
- *Is there a register?*
  Some early printed books included a register—a list of the order in which the signatures should be gathered. Registers are usually found on the last leaf of a book. If your book has a register, you might want to check it against your book's signature marks to see if they match. If there is a discrepancy, do you have any guesses about why that happened?
- *Are there multiple works bound into a single volume?*
  Some owners would bind together different works into a single volume. Such a sammelband might bring together works along a similar theme or that were printed in the same period. They could be bound near the time that they were printed and bought, or they could be bound together by a later owner. If this is a sammelband, does it seem to have an organizing principle?

Page Features

Headlines

- *Are there headlines in your book?*
  Many early printed books, like modern ones, use headlines to identify the work and to assist navigation, but not all do. Like other
  features of print, headlines are a practice that evolved over the
  development of printing.
- *What sort of information do they seem to present?*
  They might include the author's name, the title of the book, the title
  of the section, foliation, or pagination.
- *Are they consistent?*
  If there are variations, what are they? Generally headlines are
  intended to be consistent across a work, but there might be variations across sections, for instance. There might also be errors or
  other accidental variants in headlines. Sometimes variants in the
  headlines can be used to trace the order in which the book was
  printed; see the section about skeleton formes in "Printing" in Part 2.

Signature Marks

- *Does your book use signature marks?*
  You can find a refresher on what signature marks are and how they
  are used in Part 3.
- *What do they look like?*
  Do they use the alphabet to identify gatherings? Are there any
  other symbols used? Are leaves counted in arabic or roman
  numerals? Variations like these can be used to identify where a
  book was printed.
- *Are there any inconsistencies in the signatures?*
  Are there gatherings or leaves that are out of order or missing? Are
  there any interruptions in the pattern of counting gatherings? Such
  inconsistencies can offer clues as to how a book was made or evidence of later alterations to it. Can you think of any reasons why
  there are inconsistencies here?

Catchwords

- *Does your book use catchwords?*
  It probably does. Catchwords were something developed in the
  manuscript tradition, so they were generally incorporated into
  print from early on.

- *Where do the catchwords appear?*
Catchwords are nearly always at the bottom of a page in the direction line. But are they only on rectos of leaves, or on rectos and versos? If your text is set in columns, are there catchwords at the bottom of any columns? The location of catchwords is sometimes a clue as to where the book was printed.
- *Are there inconsistencies between the catchwords and the start of the text on the next page?*
Differences between catchwords and the text they're supposed to "catch" could indicate cancels or stop-press changes; differences in spelling (e.g. "dear" and "deare") are usually unimportant. Do you have explanations for any inconsistencies?

Illustrations

- *Are there illustrations in the book? Approximately how many?*
It's generally better to think of illustrations as a different category than the decorative fillers that printers use as headpieces and tailpieces or as initial letters. If your book does have illustrations, they might range in number from one to a handful to many.
- *How big are the illustrations?*
Approximations of how big they are in terms of page size can be the most useful to note at this stage. Are they full-page pictures? Quarter-page?
- *How were they made?*
Can you tell if they are woodcuts, engravings, or etchings? ("Illustrations" in Part 2 has detailed information on identifying these different processes.)
- *Have any of them been colored?*
Hand-coloring of illustrations could happen before a book was purchased or by a later owner. The presence of colored illustrations can be a sign of how a book was intended to be used and its subsequent history.

Leaves

- *Is there any evidence of leaves having been removed from the book?*
Look for stubs and irregularities in catchwords, pagination, or foliation.
- *Are there any signs of leaves having been added to the book?*
Look for leaves attached to stubs and irregularities in catchwords, pagination, or foliation. Both the removal and the addition of leaves

can happen during the book's original printing and binding process or can be signs of later owners' alterations. Are there signs that indicate whether added leaves were contemporaneous to the book's printing or came later? Do you have any sense of why the leaves were added?

Usage

Wear and Tear

- *Are there notable marks of wear or damage?*
  Common signs of wear include wormholes, water stains, torn or repaired pages, mold, foxing, and cut-out pages or sections. Damage can happen accidentally or can be the result of deliberate interventions. Sometimes what we see now as damage can be the result of earlier efforts at conservation. Slashed pages in particular can be the result of censorship.
- *Are parts of the book more worn than others?*
  The beginnings and ends of books are particularly susceptible to accidental damage, especially if the book remained unbound for any length of time. Interior sections of books that show more wear than others might have been read more often, or perhaps were displayed in a manner that exposed some leaves more than others. Do the worn or damaged parts of the book suggest anything about how the book was used?

Users' Marks

- *Are there marks left by users in the book? Where?*
  You might find marks left by readers scattered on a couple of pages, concentrated in a single section, or only on the endleaves. They might be plentiful or they might be scarce.
- *What sorts of marks do you see?*
  Would you describe them as doodles? Comments? Signatures? Crossing out text? Other marks might be manicules (pointing fingers or fists), pen trials (random marks made to get the ink flowing), pictures, colored-in initials, textual annotations, or comments unrelated to the text. Marks that strike through or strive to obliterate text could be evidence of censorship, especially if the text refers to or is about religion. Would you characterize the marks you see as working with the book, resisting the book, or neither?

- *Is it possible to tell when they were made?*
  Some inscriptions might be dated or signed. But more often it's easier to try to categorize them as roughly contemporary with the book's publication or from later centuries. You might need the assistance of a librarian to help you with recognizing these differences. (There's some guidance on dating annotations in Part 5.)

Provenance

- *Are there any marks of ownership?*
  Common provenance markings include bookplates, library shelf-marks, owners' inscriptions, bookseller descriptions, prices, and exhibition labels. With the exception of inscriptions, these are usually found on the pastedowns and endleaves of a volume; inscriptions may be found there, on the title page, or in the interior of a book. Sometimes later plates will obscure earlier ones, and later owners will cross out inscriptions of earlier ones, making them tantalizingly illegible.
- *If the marks are legible, can you identify who owned the book, when they owned it, and where they lived?*
  Do any of these owners seem surprising or notable? Do they suggest anything about the book's audiences, reception, or users? (For more on provenance see the relevant section in Part 5.)

What is image metadata?

Metadata is data about data; in this case, it's information about an image. What equipment was used to make it, how big the file is, who took the image, and where it was taken are metadata fields that are automatically captured by most cameras, camera phones, and scanners. Other information that could be recorded in an image's metadata include what the image is of, who created the object in the image, who the rights holder is, how it's licensed for use, and more technical specifications about image compression, colors, and whether the image has been modified.

Image metadata might be in a file that is attached to the image file, or it might be part of the image file itself (embedded metadata).

Digitization

The previous questions guide you through working with a book in hand. Many of those questions are similar to those you would ask when looking at a digitization of an early printed work: thinking about what content and page features appear can be done with digital images. But there are other questions that are important to ask when looking at digitizations, and this section will help you navigate working with early printed books in a digital medium. If you've been working with a book in hand, it can be interesting to find a digital version—whether of the same copy or of a different one—and compare the experience of using it. (See "Books on Screen" in Part 5 for more information about digital images and platforms.)

What is this Thing?

• *Are you working with pages or with openings?*
Images of books can depict either individual pages, sometimes edited to remove any signs of their facing pages or gutter, or full openings of two facing pages. (Images of full openings might have been edited to stitch together two separate photos of pages.) How does this choice affect how the book is used? Does it alter how the book creates meaning?

There are three main metadata standards—Exif, IPTC, and XMP—each of which captures different fields of information. Some image viewers can display all three standards, some only one or two, and some don't display any. The Wikipedia article "Comparison of metadata editors" can help you find a suitable viewer. The standards currently in use, however, are generally not designed for cultural heritage work such as imaging old books. For example, they do not always differentiate between the image's creator and the object's creator (e.g. the book's author). And libraries themselves do not have an agreed-upon standard for whether and how they might attach or embed such metadata to or in their images. In other words, you might find helpful metadata, you might find irrelevant metadata, or you might not find any metadata from the library at all. (It's important to remember that not all file types support embedded metadata, so if you were to resave your jpg file as a tiff, you would lose any embedded metadata. There's also nothing to prevent someone from overwriting or inserting metadata with incorrect information, so if it's really important that you know some details, you'll need to contact the library that imaged it.)

• *Are you looking at discrete images or a sequential series?*
Different platforms will display images of books differently, some showing images in a "book reader" presentation that displays pages in the order in which they are gathered in the book. Others show images in a random sequence that can be reordered according to different criteria. How are the images of your book presented? How does this shape its use?

• *Is the image part of a fully digitized work?*
Sometimes only a part of a book might be digitized—a single page, or only pages with illustrations, or only a section of a text. Other times an entire book will be imaged. Are you looking at a digitized book or a selection of images from a book? Can you tell why a particular selection was chosen for imaging?

Size

- *Can you tell what size the object imaged is?*
  It's much harder to tell what size something is when you're looking at a picture of it. Are there clues as to how big the book is? Is there a ruler depicted alongside it? Information displayed alongside in a catalog record? Does knowing (or not knowing) the size affect your reception of it?
- *What size is the image itself?*
  Image sizes are usually described in terms of pixels, sometimes given in height and width, sometimes described only in terms of the longest dimension of the two. (Image size is distinct from image resolution, although often higher resolution images correspond to larger images.) Do you know what size the image is that you are looking at? Does it display at the same size as it downloads, if it's available to download? Is that information provided as part of the image record or only as embedded metadata?

What's there and What's not

- *Is the binding or other housing imaged?*
  Most early printed books have survived in some sort of binding, whether contemporary or from later periods. Is the binding imaged? The endleaves?
- *Are blanks imaged?*
  Some printed works include blank pages or leaves, including on the verso of inserted engravings, or at the end of the final gathering. Does this digitization include images of blanks? Can you tell if blanks are missing?
- *Are other texts bound with this work included?*
  If your text is part of a sammelband, are the other texts that are part of this volume included in the imaging? Are they imaged but presented separately?
- *What can you see?*
  How much detail can you see? Can you compare different pieces of type? Can you see the texture of the page? Can you see watermarks or chainlines? Does the presence or absence of any of the features discussed here suggest anything about the purpose of this digitization? What uses is it intended for?

Container

- *What sort of platform contains the digitization?*
  Digital images are made available through software and programs that can present information through a wide range of methods. Is your digitized work part of a larger collection of digitized images? Is the collection based on a single institution, a geographical consortium, or a specific period?
- *What types of information are included in this platform?*
  What does this platform provide in addition to images of your work? Are there catalog records? Is there other contextual information, such as information about the work, or about the collection?
- *Is the platform openly accessible? Does it permit reuse of images?*
  Do you need a subscription to access images? Is it only accessible through an institutional affiliation? Is it open to anyone with a browser? Can you download images? Can you share images? Under what terms (personal use only, research purposes, share-alike licensing) are images available for reuse?

Manufacture

- *Is information provided about who imaged the book, when, and with what technology and financing?*
  Can you find out who took the pictures of the book (either the name of the photographer or the institution)? Do you know when the book was imaged? What equipment was used to take the images and to process them? How was the imaging paid for? Does this information suggest any context for why these images were created or how they were intended to be used?
- *Is information provided about who built the platform hosting the image, when, and with what software and financing?*
  Can you find out who built the software and platform hosting the digital images? (This is more likely to be a company than individuals' names.) Do you know when the platform was built? Is there information about how it was financed or if it is a subscription software?

Part 5

The Afterlives of Books

Books are printed at a moment in time, but they continue to exist long after their making and are sometimes remade repeatedly by later users. If part of how a book means is through what it looks like, it is helpful to know which aspects of a book's appearance can be attributed to its early creators and which to readers and owners in later periods. This part of the guide teaches you how to recognize characteristics left by those later owners and how to think about what their interventions might reveal.

The first section focuses on understanding catalog records. The second looks at physical books and the types of things you might notice if you're working with a book in front of you. And the third focuses on facsimile images of books and how pictures of books omit, alter, and reveal aspects of the physical book.

Loss Rates

Before we talk about the afterlives of books, we need to pause over one important fact: we can only study what has survived. What we know about the transmission of texts, what we deduce from bibliographic evidence, what we infer about the book trade—all of this depends on looking at books and on knowing what books were printed. But a substantial amount of the early modern printed world did not survive to the 21st century.

Why would entire print runs disappear completely? Books that were heavily used were, essentially, used up. Books like ABCs and catechisms didn't survive because they were read to tatters. Cheap print disappeared because it wasn't valued by contemporary collectors or those who immediately followed its publication. Newssheets, ballads, and pamphlets were read and perhaps passed on but

Studying Early Printed Books 1450–1800: A Practical Guide, First Edition. Sarah Werner.
© 2019 Sarah Werner. Published 2019 by John Wiley & Sons Ltd.

eventually forgotten about or discarded. Even books that might have been intended to be saved could easily be lost or destroyed over the centuries by fire, flood, mice, or human negligence.

But if books are lost, how do we know what they were? We can look at book lists and other contemporary documents and find books that are no longer extant. Catalogs of the Frankfurt Book Fair, libraries, and booksellers, and the Stationers' Registers refer to books that we can no longer find. Other documents record agreements for various jobs to print large runs of government documents and indulgences that we have no trace of today. Christophe Plantin kept a copy of every official edict he printed. Although the detailed records maintained by his shop—and still kept today—are very unusual for hand-press printers, we can guess from his records that others did similar work, even if they didn't archive their results.

Sometimes a book might provide evidence for earlier editions now missing, and by following the impression statements on the title pages, we can identify lost books. Elizabeth Jocelin's *A mothers legacie* was printed for the first time in 1624 (STC 14624); later that year, it was issued again with the identification of it being the "second impression" on its title page (STC 14624.5). The third edition followed close behind in 1625 (STC 14625), and then a sixth in 1632 (STC 14625.5) and a seventh in 1635 (STC 14625.7). Where are the fourth and fifth editions? Lost to time, presumably. *A mothers legacie* was clearly popular, otherwise it would not have been reprinted so frequently, and yet we do not have even a handful of copies for most of its editions. And if the book didn't state what impression it was on the title page, we might not even realize we were missing two runs. (See Alan Farmer's recent work along these lines, using such evidence to think through popularity and ephemera.)

It's possible to use statistical analysis to recover lost editions that aren't otherwise traceable by looking at how many extant copies survive per edition of a text. Neil Harris, for example, surveyed 366 pre-1601 editions of Italian chivalric romances. One edition had a whopping 108 extant copies, but those numbers quickly dropped off to the 206 editions that survived in only a single copy each. Using a technique called "zero graphing," Harris projected that there are around 600 editions that didn't survive at all.

Why does it matter whether bibliographers and book historians know what it missing from the surviving record? It's difficult for us to know how the book trade worked without an accurate sense of what was printed. In many ways, library collections are more representative of 19th- and 20th-century interests than of 16th- and 17th-century tastes. They are full of high-culture and high-status books that often were meant to be saved, large folios that were protected by bindings, and generally the sort of canonical works that form the backbone of literature and history studies. But those works were not the backbone of hand-press printing. If we were to build our understanding of how early print was created and sold based on only a portion of their work, we would miss the full scope of how printing shops survived and why the book trade was shaped as it was.

Catalog Records

Since most rare books libraries don't let users browse their stacks, users need to become adept at searching, browsing, and understanding catalog records in order to access collections. A library's catalog exists in large part to state what materials the library has and where they can be found. But catalogs can also provide detailed descriptions of both the ideal copy of a book and the features specific to the copy the library holds. And some catalogs are not tied to one library's holdings but to a category of books, listing all known editions and states from a period of time, for example, or of an author or printer.

If you're looking for a book at your library, the first places to check are the online and card catalogs. While books are now usually cataloged online, rare book collections at most institutions started before electronic records and so were cataloged on

Using card catalogs

If you've never used a card catalog before, don't worry—they're easy to get used to. Cards are organized in drawers which are, in turn, organized alphabetically by author or by subject, chronologically by date, or by any other system that a library finds productive. Individual cards don't have a lot of space on them and so information is usually truncated, although it can be continued onto other cards, if need be. Generally speaking, you'll find the heading at the top of the card—the author, if that's how it was ordered, or the subject or date. Below that will be the rest of the pertinent information identifying the work: author (if that wasn't the heading), title, imprint. There is often some abbreviated bibliographic information, and there might be some additional description provided. The shelfmark (or call number) usually is on the upper left of the card. Before the advent of online cataloging, some libraries would make print copies of their card catalogs for offsite researchers to use. Your local research library might, for instance, have printed copies of the catalogs of the New York Public Library. The most prominent of these—and still useful—is the *National Union Catalog of Pre-1956 Imprints*, which reproduces the cards of works printed before 1956 and held by major American and Canadian libraries.

cards. Libraries have not necessarily converted their old card catalogs to online systems; if that's the case, consulting the card catalogs and any other paper-based records is an important part of your search. Even if they have converted, sometimes there is useful information recorded on the cards that didn't make it into the online catalog, so it's worth taking a look.

Looking at a library's catalog record for a book it holds should give you roughly three categories of information: what the book is (name, title, imprint), what the general attributes of the book are (bibliographic information applicable to all copies of that book, subject matter), and holdings information (copy-specific details and shelfmark or call number). In other words, the record will contain both general information about that book and information that applies only to the copy the library owns.

The basis for a catalog record is usually the ideal copy of the book—that is, the imagined version of the book that is most perfect and complete, regardless of whether the library's copy matches it or not. One way of thinking about an ideal copy is as the final version of an edition: it has all its leaves, all the cancels, all its plates. That ideal copy is the source of the basic information about the book, such as what it is and what it should look like. Copy-specific information describes what the book the library holds actually looks like, including information like missing leaves, the state of relevant variants, the presence of marginalia or provenance markers, and a description of the binding. Providing detailed copy-specific information is a time-consuming process that requires book-in-hand cataloging; not all libraries have the resources to create such records, and the amount of detail you encounter will range across the scale. Even without such information in the record, however, you can get a good sense of a book's features.

Need to save a link to an online record?

Most catalogs provide something identified as a "permalink," "persistent record," or "durable URL" that should be used if you need to share or cite an online catalog record. It's usually not a good idea to copy and paste from the address in your browser, since those URLs often contain elements that make them time-out and become unusable.

Identification: Author, Title, Imprint

The "author" or sometimes just "name" listed is usually the standardized form of the name of the person who created the work. If a work

If my book doesn't have an author, where is its record?

One of the advantages of computer cataloging is that you can look up an item under almost any field. But records usually have a "main entry" that determines where a record is filed, and "added entries" that contain additional information. An analogy might be how an index to a book works. You might look up "red" and find an entry that says "see colors," and when you go to "colors" you will find the page numbers you're looking for; in this example, "colors" is the main entry and "red" is an added entry. The main entry for a record is usually the author's name; if there's no author, the main entry becomes the title of the work.

Looking for a Bible?

Religious texts can be particularly tricky to find in a catalog. What we commonly refer to as the King James Bible carries the printed title of *The Holy Bible, conteyning the Old Testament, and the New: newly translated out of the originall tongues: & with the former translations diligently compared and reuised, by his Maiesties speciall co[m]mandement. Appointed to be read in churches.* and is given a uniform title of "Bible. English. Authorized." (STC 2217). On the one hand, neither of these are titles for which you might first be inclined to search. But on the other, identifying Bibles by the language in which they are written and what version they are is a logical way of organizing them. (The King James was created on the orders of King James, and so the "authorized" version that was to be used in churches.) One useful resource for working with Bibles is the *Historical Catalogue of Editions of the English Bible 1525–1961*, published by the British and Foreign Bible Society.

has multiple authors, often only one is listed in this field. These names are usually standardized according to centralized databases known as authority files. This standardization helps users navigate the various spellings, name changes, and pseudonyms used by writers. For instance, if you search for Mary Sidney (the name by which modern scholars often refer to this author and translator of early modern English works), you might be redirected to "Pembroke, Mary Sidney Herbert, Countess of, 1561–1621." Translations and editions sometimes present an additional spin on name searches. Mary Sidney's translation of Philippe de Mornay's *Excellent discours de la vie et de la mort* (STC 18138) is typically listed with de Mornay as the primary author and Sidney identified in the "associated names" section.

Multiple titles for a work are often provided in a catalog record—the title under which it was published, variant titles, and a uniform title by which the work is commonly known. For example, the collection of poems compiled and published by Richard Tottel has the proper title of *Songes and sonettes, written by the right honorable Lorde Henry Haward late Earle of Surrey, and other* (STC 13861), but it's more typically known as *Tottel's miscellany*, which is given as a uniform title. Sometimes a catalog record will provide variant titles, which are usually titles that appear in the book's headlines, but could also be alternate names by which the book is known.

Imprint information can also be provided in a variety of ways. Sometimes a catalog will provide the name, location, and date of printing in the format of "Place: Publisher, Date," mirroring how we cite that information today. If that's the case, the exact language of the imprint statement as it appears in the book is often provided in the notes. For example, if you're looking at a record for Erasmus's Greek-Latin translation of the New Testament (VD16 B 4196), you might see the publication information as "Basel: Froben, 1516" with a note reproducing the exact imprint as seen in the colophon, "Basileae: In aedibus Ioannis Frobenij Hammelburgensis, mense Februario anno MDXVI." Alternatively, the record might use the language of the imprint statement without listing its entirety: "Basileae, in aedibus Johann Froben, 1516." (The Latin phrase "in aedibus" means "in the shop of;" "Ionnis Frobenij" is the Latinized form of "Johann Froben." RBMS provides a handy list of common phrases found in Latin imprints that can be useful to consult; the CERL Thesaurus provides variant names of people and places, along with links to other useful information. Details about these resources, and others of use in understanding cataloging information, can be found in Appendix 1, "Catalog and Imprint Resources.")

Sometimes the details of a book's publication aren't provided in the book itself but are supplied by the cataloger in square brackets. A work might have been printed anonymously but later identified, or the location might be misidentified and then corrected. For example, *Robert Earle of Essex his ghost, sent from Elizian.: to the nobility, gentry, and communaltie of England.* has, as mentioned in Part 3, this imprint statement on the title page: "Printed in Paradise. 1624." The record of the ESTC (English Short Title Catalogue) for this work supplies additional information about the location and name of the printer: "Printed in Paradise [i.e. London : by John Beale?], 1624." (ESTC S101222). The question mark indicates that Beale is probably the printer but not certainly so.

If imprint information is missing from the title page and there's no colophon, a catalog record will indicate its absence, often with the Latin abbreviations "s.l." for "sine loco" ("without location"), "s.n." for "sine nominee" ("without name"), and "s.a." for "sine anno" ("without year"). Cataloging practices are moving away from the Latin to the slightly more user-friendly abbreviations "n.p." for "no place" or "no printer" and "n.d." for "no date."

Description: What it Looks Like, What it's About

Catalog records also provide information about the general physical characteristics of a book. Based on an ideal copy, it's a way of further identifying the work under discussion. For readers versed in interpreting catalog statements, it's also a way of beginning to imagine what a book might look like.

The specifics of how a record states the physical description of a book vary across cataloging standards, but some basic principles are observed. Records will usually provide a description of how many pages or leaves are in a book. Typically this statement indicates the series of page or leaf numbers in the book, giving the last number in the series and placing unnumbered pages or leaves in square brackets. For example, the book printed in Paradise described above has the pagination statement "[2], 18, [4], 11, [1] p."—that is, there are two unnumbered pages, followed by pages numbered 1 through 18, followed by 4 unnumbered pages, then pages numbered 1 through 11, and ending with one unnumbered page. If a book is foliated, that will be reflected in its statement with the abbreviation "ff." for "folios." And if a book's pages and leaves aren't numbered at all, the statement will supply the count in brackets, as in this description of Petrarch's Italian poetry, edited by Pietro Bembo and printed by Aldus Manutius in 1501 (EDIT16 36111): "[192] c." ("c." is the abbreviation for the Italian word *carte*, the term used for leaves in a book). Some cataloging standards require simply listing the number of leaves, regardless of whether they're numbered.

The general description might also include information on whether there are illustrations, what format the book is, and its size. The ESTC record for John Seller's 1677 collection of astronomical works, *Atlas cælestis*, includes this description: "[2], 72 p., [75] leaves of plates (some folded, some double): charts, diags., maps, ports.; 8°" (ESTC R12842). In other words, this book begins with two unnumbered pages, followed by 72 sequentially numbered pages, with 75 unnumbered leaves of plates of charts, diagrams, maps, and portraits, and the book is in an octavo format.

A catalog might include a collation statement, a sequence that describes the gatherings of a book. And some include a book's bibliographic fingerprint, a way of identifying editions and states. Depending on the catalog, this information might be labeled "fingerprint" or "LOC" or "STCN." (See "Collation Formulas" and "Fingerprints" later in this section for explanation of these terms.)

Catalog records can also provide additional general information about a book, ranging from noting where supplied information about the imprint came from, to describing the work's contents and relationship to other editions.

A record might also provide citations or references to other sources that serve as the basis for the record or that provide important additional information that can be helpful for your research. Such sources have typically been provided in shortened form. The ESTC record for Caxton's 1477 *Canterbury Tales* provides these citations: "Duff, 87; GW, 6585; STC (2nd ed), 5082; Needham, P. Printer & the pardoner, Cx 17." Knowing what these abbreviations refer to can take some sleuthing. New American cataloging rules call for such citations to be provided in full, but you will still frequently come across abbreviated citations. The RBMS site Standard Citation Forms for Rare Materials Cataloging offers a search function that can help you identify citations. With a bit of searching, you can turn "Duff" into E. Gordon Duff's 1917 book *Fifteenth Century English Books: A Bibliography of Books and Documents Printed in England and of Books for the English Market Printed Abroad* and "GW" into *Gesamtkatalog der Wiegendrucke,* the German union catalog for incunabula.

Being familiar with the citation or reference field can also help you when you want to find a record for an item you know in a different catalog. You can look up any of the STC or Wing references I've provided in this guide by looking them up in the ESTC in the "citation note" field (you'll need to use the advanced search option to find it). Or if you want to find non-Italian holdings listed for a book in EDIT16, you can search the USTC for that reference number in their citation field. (A description of and links to these catalogs, and other important ones for the hand-press period, can be found in Appendix 1.)

Catalog records might include information about the subject of a work. These subject headings are usually derived from a centralized source and often follow the same principles as subject headings for contemporary books. In the United States, that means following Library of Congress subject headings, which are organized to proceed from general subject to narrower fields. Augustine Vincent's correction-laden work *A discouerie of errours* (STC 24756) has as its subject headings in ESTC "Heraldry—Great Britain—Early works to 1800," "Great Britain—Kings and rulers—Early works to 1800," and "Nobility—Great Britain—Early works to 1800." A quick perusal of the subject headings can give you a sense of what the work is about. And each of those headings can be followed to find other works that share that topic.

Holding Details: Provenance, Copy-Specific Details, Shelfmarks

The final category of information a catalog can provide is details about the copy the library holds. If everything prior to this is applicable to all copies of that book, this category is true only for the copy or copies at the library. At a minimum, a record should indicate a shelfmark or a call number for the book; if the library owns multiple copies of a book, it will usually include the shelfmark for each copy.

If the cataloger was able to spend time closely examining the library's copy in the process of creating a record, it might include details about what the book looks like, such as how it's bound, whether there are manuscript annotations, if any print variants are included, and who previous owners were. Such book-in-hand cataloging is valuable for researchers, but it is time-consuming and not all libraries can create such detailed records.

Union Catalogs and Shared Cataloging

Catalogs like GW and ESTC are not linked to an institution's holdings but are union catalogs that provide records for groups of books regardless of where they are held—incunabula, in the case of GW, or books printed in English or in the British Isles and British colonies before 1801, in the case of ESTC. While union catalogs often list institutions that hold the relevant books, such lists are usually self-reported and not necessarily exhaustive. Smaller libraries, for instance, are often not included in such listings, nor are private owners. (See the following section, "What's not in a Catalog," for more on this important component of using catalogs.)

Union catalogs often serve as the basis for the ideal copy described in institutional holdings. Shared cataloging—in which one entity shares its catalog records with libraries—has been a standard part of the cataloging workflow in many libraries. WorldCat is a union catalog maintained by members of the OCLC (Online Computer Library Center, a library cooperative) that is the basis for much English-language cataloging. A library might simply incorporate the OCLC WorldCat records into their own catalog, or they might add to those records with copy-specific or other details. If a member library updates the OCLC record with, for instance, a more detailed physical description or additional notes about the book, that record is then updated in the OCLC database for other libraries to draw on.

One aspect of such shared cataloging that sometimes goes overlooked by researchers is that a library's catalogers are not always individually making decisions about a record's claims. For instance, if the ESTC identifies an undated book as having been published in 1622, any library drawing on the ESTC's records will also identify it as a 1622 publication. In other words, the reason so many catalog records for English-language hand-press books describe works in identical terms is because they are all derived from the same source.

What's not in a Catalog?

Just as important as knowing how to use a catalog is knowing what's not in it. Catalogs can only list books that they know of—that is, books that have been found, identified, and reported to catalogers. Most libraries have a backlog of items in their collections that have not yet been fully cataloged; some libraries will include these partial records in their catalogs, others will list them only in their accession records (files usually for internal use tracking purchases and donations).

Union catalogs can, of course, only include items that have been cataloged, but also only those at participating libraries. Similarly, catalogs that record the locations of items—like the ESTC—only include the holdings of the libraries they've checked, and those libraries tend to be the prominent ones. Projects like Renaissance Books, Midwestern Libraries, which has been submitting its findings of ESTC books for inclusion, have expanded the catalog's holdings records to a wider range of institutions. But it's important to remember that catalogs like ESTC and EDIT16 don't list all known copies of an item but only locations of copies that they know of.

Finally, not all catalogs intend to list all things. In fact, nearly all have limits as to what is eligible for inclusion and what is not. Catalogs of an institution provide records only for those items at that institution; you shouldn't expect to find a book owned by Bryn Mawr College in the catalog for the University of Glasgow. Catalogs of a subject or a period of course only include items related to their focus, so if a work was printed in the 18th century, you won't find it in EDIT16, which only covers 16th-century Italian works. But they can also define those items in ways that are important to know; the GW, for instance, records incunabula but it excludes broadsides, so indulgences aren't listed, even though they are among the earliest printed texts. (The descriptions of catalogs in Appendix 1 include further information about what they do and do not cover.)

Collation Formulas

In many catalogs or descriptions of hand-press books, a collation formula is provided to identify the structure of the book. To the untrained eye, it merely looks like a series of letters and numbers. But once you know how to read the formula, it can provide helpful information about the book before you even look at it.

Here's a sample formula for a straightforward book to get us started:

$$4^\circ: a^2, b-g^4, h^2$$

Not all leaves

Collation formulas don't record all leaves in an ideal copy of a book but only those leaves printed on sheets that went through the common press. In other words, inserted plates from a rolling press don't appear in formulas. The title page of the First Folio, which has an engraved portrait of Shakespeare, appears in the collation discussed below because that leaf includes both an engraving and letterpress text.

The first bit of information before the colon tells us the format of the book—in this case, a quarto. What follows the colon tells us the sequence of gatherings that make up the book, providing the signature of the gathering and the number of leaves in it. In this book, the first gathering is signed "a" and it has two leaves. It is followed by six gatherings signed sequentially "b" through "g," each with four leaves in the gathering. The final gathering is signed "h" and has two leaves.

All collation formulas follow the same pattern, even if the information they provide is more complicated. Here's another example:

$$4^\circ: \S^4, a-q^8 (\pm q2), r^4$$

This describes the book as being in a quarto format (4°), the first gathering of which is four leaves signed with a section mark ($\S^4$), followed by 16 gatherings signed alphabetically "a" through "q" with each gathering consisting of eight leaves ($a-q^8$; remember that signatures follow the 23-letter alphabet, so this includes a gathering signed either "i" or "j" but not two gatherings), followed by a gathering labeled "r" consisting of four leaves (r^4). The second leaf of the q gathering has a leaf (the cancelland) which has been replaced by the cancel ($\pm q2$). (If the cancelland had been removed but not replaced, it would be signaled with a minus sign: $-q2$.)

Sometimes collation formulas can get very complex, as in this for Shakespeare's First Folio:

$$2°: \ ^{\pi}A^6 \left(^{\pi}A1+1, \ ^{\pi}A5+1.2 \right), A–2B^6, 2C^2, a–g^6, \ ^{\chi}2g^8,$$
$$h–v^6, x^4, \text{"gg3.4"} \left(\pm\text{"gg3"} \right), \P–2\P^6, 3\P1, 2a–2f^6, 2g^2,$$
$$\text{"Gg6"}, 2h^6, 2k–3b^6$$

As a beginning bibliographer, what's probably most useful for you to know about formulas like this is that they are describing a book that had some complex variations happen as it was being printed. But, if you're curious, here's what's going on with the parts of the formula we haven't yet learned. The superscript π preceding the initial gathering differentiates the preliminaries from the first gathering of the main text since, in this book, both are signed "A." The + is used to indicate the presence of leaves that are not part of the signed sheet but that are inserted into the gathering. A period joining two numbers indicates that those two leaves are conjugate (if they were adjacent but not conjugate leaves inserted after A5, they would be indicated with a comma: A5+1,2). The superscript χ is used to indicate a gathering that uses the same signature as another gathering in the middle of the book; it's typically placed before the second of those gatherings but sometimes before the first if it's clear that the first was inserted after the second was printed. And the quotation marks around some of the gatherings indicate how the gathering has been signed by the printer, even though such signatures do not conform to the usual pattern of the book.

So to translate this collation formula into readable language: This book is a folio. It begins with a six-leaf gathering signed "A" that has a single leaf inserted after the first leaf and two conjoined leaves inserted following the fifth leaf. Following that are six-leaf gatherings signed sequentially "A" through "BB," and then a two-leaf gathering signed "CC." Next is a series of six-leaf gatherings signed sequentially "a" through "g," followed by an eight-leaf gathering signed "gg," then a series of six-leaf gatherings signed sequentially "h" through "v," and then a four-leaf gathering signed "x." Next is a gathering signed "gg3" and "gg4" that consists of two conjoined leaves of which "gg3" is a cancel replacing the original cancelland. Next are two six-leaf gatherings signed first with one pilcrow (¶) and then with two, followed by a single leaf signed with three pilcrows. A six-leaf series signed sequentially "aa" through "ff" is next, followed by a two-leaf gathering signed "gg," then a six-leaf gathering signed "Gg." Finally is a six-leaf gathering signed "hh" and then a series of six-leaf gatherings signed sequentially "kk" through "bbb."

Even without knowing the history of this book, you can get a sense of its organization and see that something happened during its printing. For instance, the fact that the CC gathering is only two leaves, instead of six, and followed by a new sequence of signatures suggests that the transition in signatures marks a change in sections of the book. (Indeed, this marks the shift from the Comedies to the Histories.) And the "gg3.4" gathering interrupts the otherwise orderly sequence, as does the following series of pilcrows, raising both the question of what is the interruption and why are the "gg" leaves separate from the pilcrow sequence. (The pilcrow gatherings are for *Troilus and Cressida*, a play that was only added to the collection after printing had begun. The "gg3" cancel is the Prologue of the play, which was originally omitted.) The printing history of the First Folio is complex, but even without knowing the details, you can get a sense of it from the formula.

The key thing to remember when you're reading collation formulas is that what is described is the bibliographer's notion of the ideal copy of the book, not necessarily what you might have in hand. For instance, a formula might describe the book as having a cancel, while the book you're looking at still has the original cancelland. (Sometimes collation formulas are used to describe a specific copy of a book, not an ideal copy, but that usage is usually noted as such.) As a beginning bibliographer, the basic principle to remember in creating a collation is that you need to identify the format of the book, and then describe the sequence of gatherings. If you do need to record a collation, Bowers's *Principles of Bibliographical Description* is the standard source for the practice for the hand-press period.

Fingerprints

Bibliographic fingerprinting is a way of identifying a specific setting of a text with a unique code drawn from different, semi-random details of the text. It can be used, for example, to identify different editions of a book, even when the book is missing its title page or has a misleading imprint. The essential premise is that every time a book is reset, even if the text remains the same, the precise arrangement of type shifts. By recording specific aspects of a setting, a bibliographer can differentiate between different states, even if from outward appearance two books seem the same.

There are two dominant systems of fingerprinting in current use. The LOC system came out of the London-Oxford-Cambridge project to create a union catalog and is primarily used in Britain, Italy, and Germany; you might come across examples of it in EDIT16 and VD16/17. LOC fingerprinting is based on characters of the last and penultimate lines on a set group of pages: the first printed recto following the title page, the fourth printed recto following that, the first recto numbered 13, and its verso. On the first three of those pages, you record the final two characters in the last two lines, excluding the direction line; on the verso, you record the first two characters of the last two lines. (The actual rules are a bit more complicated but are spelled out in the LOC fingerprinting manual, *Fingerprints, Empreintes, Impronte.*) The fingerprint concludes with an indication of how the third page was determined and with the date of publication and an indication of how that date was determined.

So if you were to see this fingerprint in a catalog:

chde nss= n.rt DuWa (3) 1611(R)

you would interpret as follows: The characters from each leaf are grouped into four, separated by spaces, so, for example, you'd know that "ch" are the last two characters of penultimate line on the first printed recto following the title page and "de" are the last two on the final line of that page. (The last character on the final line is actually "ē," but the fingerprint uses the base letter in its formula, dropping accents or abbreviations, so it's represented here as "e.") The second grouping is taken from the fourth printed recto after the first, and so on, as laid out above. The "(3)" indicates that the third and fourth groups are taken from a page numbered 13 and its verso (as opposed to some of the other ways of finding this leaf). And the last bit of information is the date that the work was published (1611) with an "(R)" to indicate that the date was given in roman numerals.

The work I used to create this fingerprint was a 1611 edition of Anna Bijns's refrains, *Gheestelyck refereyn boeck, verclarende die moghentheydt Gods, ende Christus ghenade, ouer die sondighe menschen* (STCV 6502678). Since the book is published in Antwerp, it's not surprising that the STCV doesn't use a LOC fingerprint to identify it but instead the Dutch formula. The Dutch or STCN fingerprinting method is used, as the name suggests, primarily by Dutch and Belgian bibliographers for the STCN and STCV projects. It records the placement of signature marks as they are aligned to the text directly above it on a set group of pages: the first and last of the preliminaries, the main text, and any text that comes after the main text. This information is preceded by a six-digit number giving the date of the imprint and the format. (A full description of this methodology can be found in P.C.A. Vriesema's article.)

So the STCN fingerprint for the same Bijns book is as follows:

161108 - b1 A2 n$be : b2 P5 tez

The first six digits show the imprint date and the format (a 1611 octavo). Because there are no preliminary materials in the book, the next set of information (b1) shows the first signature mark of the main text (A2) and the characters above it (n$be—the $ is used to indicate a space). The next set (b2) shows the last signature mark of the main text (P5) and the characters above that (tez). And since there is no appendix or other material following the main text, the formula stops there.

Neil Harris's excellent look at the history and use of fingerprinting includes a detailed account of the pros and cons of the different methods; it's a good place to start exploring the value and shortcomings of fingerprinting. But the most important thing for a beginning bibliographer to know is how to interpret the fingerprints in catalogs. (If you want to look at a copy of Bijns to try this yourself, you can find a digital facsimile at Ghent University Library: http://lib.ugent.be/en/catalog/rug01:000830829.)

Books in Hand

Differentiating Between Early and Later Characteristics

All books that have survived from the hand-press period will carry some sort of physical characteristics left by later owners. Even the most pristine-looking books bear the traces of interventions; indeed, sometimes books look pristine because pages have been bleached by later owners. These interventions can be made by users who wanted to mark their ownership of the book, by booksellers or collectors wanting to increase its value, by conservators trying to repair or preserve it, or by institutions hoping to prevent theft. All contribute to a book's history and to what we can learn not only about that individual copy but about larger stories of cultural value. But when you're studying a book's creation, it is important to be able to differentiate between what a book looked like when it was first produced and what changes were made to it by later users.

Bindings and Endleaves

The most frequent place in which you will find changes made to a book is in the binding and endleaves. In the hand-press period, of course, books were often sold unbound, leaving it to their buyers to bind if they desired. And there are certainly books that have survived in period bindings, in paper wrappers, and unbound. But many hand-press books were completely or partially rebound in later centuries, sometimes because the original bindings were worn and sometimes because an owner wanted a fancier binding.

The hinges and spine of a binding are the elements most often in need of repair—the simple wear and tear of opening and closing the binding makes them prone to damage. It's possible for a book to be rebacked or rejointed—to have only the spine or the hinges replaced with new material (usually without disturbing the sewing structure of the book). Such repairs are typically done with the same material as the original binding, but if you look closely, you can usually see that the color or the textures don't quite match.

Like the joints and the spine, a book's endleaves are frequently altered by owners. Early and later owners might have removed the original endleaves for scrap paper or simply because they didn't see them as necessary. Endleaves are also often replaced when binding repairs are being done, and if the entire binding is replaced, so are the endleaves. It's possible to recognize later endleaves just by looking carefully at the paper. Look to see if it's wove paper or if it's decorated in a style that postdates the book; paper marbled with a spot pattern, for example, didn't emerge until the middle of the 18th century, and so wouldn't be part of the original binding of a 15th-century publication.

If the entire binding has been replaced, it should in theory be easy to spot because the styles of bookbinding are always changing. Even if the new binding is intended to look like the style of the original, tools and techniques differ and such differences can be spotted by an expert eye. Developing that expert eye, however, takes some time and a lot of handling of books. There are some obvious clues that can help you notice a binding that significantly postdates the book's origins, including binder's stamps and labels—small markers naming the binder on the turn-ins or pastedowns of the binding. Catalogs will also sometime include information about the binding in their records. And there are books and online resources that have plenty of pictures of bindings characteristic of different periods that can help you begin to recognize them.

Original bindings could also be modified without being replaced. A book could have lettering added to the spine or a later owner's coat of arms could be stamped onto the binding.

The more important it is, the less likely it is to have its original binding

One of the most obvious clues that a book is likely to have been rebound in the 19th or 20th centuries is if it is a book that would have been seen by collectors as prestigious. Shakespeare's works, for instance, have nearly always been rebound, as have other works central to literary canons.

Different than rebinding is what has happened to many, if not most, sammelbände. Although 15th-, 16th-, and 17th-century owners of books often bound books together into a single volume, later owners preferred texts to be discrete. Sometimes books were disbound because a book seller or collector thought only one or two of them were valuable. Sometimes the texts bound together defied later notions of order, perhaps because the texts included multiple genres or because the book mixed print and manuscript. Or a sammelband might have been disbound because it was in need of conservation, and once apart it was decided to rebind the texts as discrete books.

Regardless of the reason for such changes, it is often difficult to know that the book you're looking at was once part of a sammelband. Obvious clues would include an endleaf listing a series of works, a binder's note describing treatment, or a catalog record listing linked items. But not all disbound sammelbände will have these records. A number written on the title page might indicate its order in a series bound together, but it might also refer to a bookseller's inventory, or an owner's annotation. Jeffrey Knight's *Bound to Read* explores the practices of binding together multiple texts into a single volume and of remaking those volumes into discrete works and argues that such practices helped shape modern categories of literature and libraries.

Page Interventions

Paper is also vulnerable to damage. The first and last leaves and gatherings of a book are especially likely to have become torn or to be missing. Especially if the book was unbound for any period of time, those leaves take the brunt of a book's handling; even in bound books, those are the leaves that bear the stress of opening and closing the volume. Leaves in the middle of a book can become torn from regular use, especially at the fore-edge where users are most likely to grab the leaf to turn it. Pages that were frequently read can become grubby and stained, iron gall ink used for annotations can eat through the paper, and pieces of the leaf can be torn out or cut to remove particularly desirable parts (e.g. illuminations and illustrations) or passages that have been censored.

Paper can also suffer damage from water, mold, foxing, and pests. Water will of course weaken paper and stain it, although it won't necessarily affect printed or manuscript ink. In humid conditions, mold can attack paper and bindings, leaving behind stains. (By the time most books end up in library use, they should no longer have active mold colonies, but mold is something that collections are always on the lookout for.) Foxing—the appearance of reddish-brown spots—comes from poorly sized paper or a chemical imbalance from bleaching and is a relatively common sight on books. Mice like to gnaw on paper and to use it for their nests. And insects can bore holes through paper and wood and eat away large areas of leaves. Any of this damage can come at any point in a book's history.

There are a range of techniques used to repair torn pages, most of which are easy to spot. Tears in pages can be held together by adhesives, while holes can be filled in with stuff or replacement paper. Conservation techniques change over the years and sometimes you can date a treatment by its methodology. In the 19th and early 20th centuries, paper that was degraded was sometimes strengthened by a process known as silking—a silk gauze was pasted to the leaf to keep it from falling apart while still allowing the text to be read. You can still find books with silked leaves, but it's a conservation practice that is no longer followed, since over time the silking can actually cause further problems.

Standards of what is considered a defect in a book have also changed over time. Many libraries now value the presence of users' marginalia, but earlier collectors had a strong preference for "clean" copies without any such marks. In an effort to create clean copies, books were sometimes washed with bleach to remove manuscript marginalia. Often such washing left behind illegible traces of the annotations, a frustrating experience for today's researcher who might be interested in how earlier users read the book. Washing can be an important aspect of paper conservation, especially for stabilizing ink damage or getting rid of mold. But bleaching to get rid of earlier users' marks is no longer a common practice.

The desire of earlier owners for clean copies also sometimes resulted in aggressively trimmed text blocks, so that margins and their annotations were eliminated. Those pages could be bound as is or inlaid into blank paper to create clean margins. Cutting off marginalia could also happen by accident when a book was rebound by a later owner; the preference for creating an even text block when binding sometimes meant that marginalia, headlines, and direction lines could end up trimmed.

Users' Marks

Trying to work out which manuscript marks left on a book came from early users rather than later ones can be a frustrating experience, if also a valuable one. Renaissance readers might have left annotations on the text, doodles in the margins, inscriptions on the endleaves and title pages, and random commentary in blank spaces. Later owners might have left their own commentary, doodles, and inscriptions. How might you tell them apart? One quick indication is spelling. Spelling was more fluid in the Renaissance than it is today, and standardization happened over the course of the 18th century. If the annotation you're reading seems like it's pretty much spelling words as you would today, that's a sign it might be from after the Renaissance. Language can also sometimes be a clue. Latin was a common language for scholarship in the 15th, 16th, and early 17th centuries, and Latin inscriptions are more likely to be from those periods than from the 19th or 20th centuries.

Handwriting is also a clue, albeit one that takes some training to be able to infer period reliably. Early styles of writing, such as the secretary hand used in England primarily in the 16th and 17th centuries, formed letters in a way that is noticeably different than the way we write today. If you familiarize yourself with particularly distinct secretary letterforms like "c," "e," and "r," that can help you categorize when the marginalia was written. However, early users also wrote in italic and roman hands that look more like our own, so be wary of assigning a date on that basis. (Resources about paleography—the study of old handwriting—are listed in Appendix 1.)

Booksellers and librarians also leave marks in books, albeit on the endleaves and usually in pencil. These are typically notes about the condition of the book, pricing codes, and shelfmarks. (See "Provenance" later in this part for more information.)

What we can learn—and can't learn—from users' annotations is a study of growing interest. William Sherman's *Used Books* is a good place to start exploring how English users marked up their books in the Renaissance and how later collectors saw them.

Inserting and Removing Leaves

One of the hardest interventions to note without careful examination is the 19th-century practice of perfecting books. Books that were seen as imperfect—missing pages or having damaged pages—were made perfect by inserting pages from other copies. While at first glance such a book might look complete, it is actually made up of leaves from different books ("made-up" or "sophisticated" are other terms for perfected). But close examination can sometimes reveal slight differences that identify the inserted leaves. Paper that is a different color or texture, wormholes that don't pass through adjacent leaves, or leaves that are a different size are signs that they might be from a different copy. Usually such perfections are not intended to deceive a user but stem from a belief that having all the text of a book is better than having only the leaves from a single copy.

Sometimes a book will be perfected by adding facsimile leaves instead of originals from different copies. In some cases, pen-and-ink facsimile copies of the replaced leaf are so meticulous that at first glance you might mistake them for an original. In the mid-19th century, John Harris produced such accurate facsimiles at the request of the British Museum that the librarians weren't always able to identify them; Harris was subsequently ordered to sign his work to prevent this problem.

A book might have blank leaves added to it so that an owner has adequate room to add in his own notes or illustrations. Such interleaving happened both in the early modern period and in later centuries; the best way to tell when the intervention happened is to examine the paper. The practice of adding in leaves and pictures was part of book ownership from its early years. But thanks to the 1769 publication of James Granger's *Biographical History of England* (ESTC T90309), which included blank leaves for the addition of portraits, such practice became popular in the late 18th and 19th centuries. Grangerizing, as it came to be known, could be done professionally or by the owner.

Some books also faced the opposite tactic: leaves were removed from the book. Books with maps and illustrations were particularly susceptible to being broken up. Owners might want the pictures for their own use or dealers might think the parts were more valuable than the whole.

Provenance

If you're interested in how a book has been used over time, you'll want to get a sense of who owned it in the past. Studying provenance is a field unto itself; the best guide for British work is David Pearson's *Provenance Research in Book History*. The focus of provenance studies has often been on association copies—items that have been owned or used by someone famous. But a book's history includes all former owners of a book, famous or not. If you are interested in patterns of book use, the full provenance history of a book (to the extent it's recorded) is of interest. This section describes some of the basic characteristics you might see in a book that will lead you toward its provenance.

Bookplates, Labels, and Stamps

Many owners paste bookplates onto the front pastedown or endleaves to mark their ownership. They are typically rectangular pieces of printed paper with the owner's name, whether an individual or a library. They might include a motto, an emblem, or a coat of arms. An owner might instead use a book label, a small slip of paper with only the owner's name. Some owners use leather rather than paper plates.

Sometimes later owners will paste their plates on top of an earlier owner's plate or label, akin to how a current owner might strike through the name of a previous owner before inscribing the book. More typical is adding a new plate without obscuring an earlier one, since provenance can be part of a book's interest. Such plates are collectors' items in their own right, and there are many library collections of them and books reproducing them.

Sometimes an owner or, more typically, an institution will mark a book with an inked, blind, or perforating stamp. Library stamps usually appear on endleaves and title pages, and sometimes key internal pages. They serve not only to identify ownership but to deter theft.

Bookseller's Marks

Booksellers often leave marks on the books they sell that describe the book, confirm its collation, or indicate its price. Such marks are usually in pencil and on the front or back endleaves. For instance, a note might comment on the perceived scarcity of the book or on its physical condition.

There can also be marks that are deliberately inscrutable. Price codes are used by booksellers to record the price paid for a book without revealing that information to potential buyers. The nine- or ten-letter keyword allows a dealer to substitute letters for numbers that can then only be cracked by those in the know. To outside observers, the price code looks like gibberish. Ian Jackson (writing under the pseudonym Exhumation, his own price code) explains the practice of price codes in further detail and provides examples, primarily from those sellers who are no longer in the business.

Sometimes a buyer will paste in the bookseller's or auction catalog description after purchase. These can be helpful in learning the perceived desirable features of the book, and sometimes in identifying the price paid for the book. Depending on the level of cataloging at the holding library, the descriptions can also point to bibliographical features that might otherwise be unnoted. But such descriptions should also be taken with a grain of salt, since the desire to make a book into a desirable commodity can sometimes lead to inflated claims of scarcity or provenance.

Library Marks

Libraries leave a range of marks on the books they own. Some of these are marks of ownership, like the plates and stamps noted above. There can also be shelfmarks or call numbers penciled in, typically on the rear pastedown. Sometimes there are annotations on the title page; if the author is identified only by initials or a pseudonym, the standard name might be written in.

Libraries often keep files of their purchasing records and related provenance information separate from the book; if you want to know more about how your library acquired the book, ask the staff.

Books on Screen

Looking at Digital Objects

Libraries are increasingly creating and sharing digital images of their rare materials, a trend that is likely to continue as digital access grows in response to user demand. But there is little agreement on what it means to provide digital facsimiles of books, whether in terms of how such images are created, how access is provided, or what uses are permitted. The most established collections of digital facsimiles of hand-press books—Early English Books Online (EEBO) and Eighteenth-Century Collections Online (ECCO)—are commercial products that are expensive and don't offer high-resolution color images, although they are easy to navigate and fairly comprehensive. Individual libraries have been digitizing their own collections, usually providing free access through their own platforms or through geographical consortia. And both Google Books and Internet Archive have created digitization programs that image rare materials and offer them through their sites.

Print facsimiles

The creation of facsimiles pre-dates digital technologies, and print facsimiles have long been helpful for researchers. A print facsimile can be easier to use, since it's in the familiar form of a book, but a high-resolution digital facsimile usually provides a more richly detailed view of the item.

This range of digital options is a boon to the researcher—it's possible to see examples of early printed books at any time of day from any computer with internet access. It can even be possible to find the specific edition you're looking to read and sometimes—albeit rarely—the specific copy you're interested in. Given that many early printed works do not exist in modern editions, reading them either with the original in hand or as facsimiles is often the only option. And given how few extant copies there are of many books, and how expensive and time-consuming it can be to travel to libraries to see them, the ability to look them up online enables research that might not otherwise be possible.

But digital images of books are not the books themselves. There are both drawbacks and advantages to working with them, but a user first has to be aware of what they are looking at and how it came to be.

Digital Images

The first thing to note when looking at a digital reproduction of an early printed book is what is shown and what is omitted. Many older images, for instance, didn't include bindings (EEBO usually does not); some didn't even include the blank sides of leaves in the text block (ECCO omits blank pages). It should be fairly obvious to tell if the binding has been imaged—it's either there or it's not there. (Even if a book is unbound, an image of it should show that the first page doesn't have another page or wrapper facing it.) Identifying whether blank leaves or pages are missing from a digital facsimile is a bit trickier if you don't know what to look for. But if there are leaves missing from a gathering or if images jump suddenly from the recto of a page to another recto instead of a verso, that's a clue.

There are also important choices made about how the book is shown. Are the images of single pages or of page openings? Working with a book on the table in front of us, we only ever view openings, unless you actively cover up the facing page or you are looking at a single leaf that isn't part of a codex. But digital images often present books as a series of pages, disrupting the sense of meaning that is generated by the interplay across the book opening and creating a different sense of proceeding through its text. If the book is shown as a series of openings, can you view the fore-edge of the volume and get a sense of the book's heft? If you're reading a book in hand, you can tell immediately where you are in it by locating yourself in its depth—if you're at the beginning of the text, the bulk of pages will still be ahead of you.

Almost always, there are details that you cannot see in a facsimile of a book that you would be able to in the book itself. Can you see chain lines and watermarks? Can you identify the page's texture? Can you note the gradations of the paper's color? It is possible to image all of these things, if the imager chooses (or is directed to). Raking light can show the texture of a page, and backlighting and other techniques can show watermarks. But most facsimiles of books prioritize easy reading of the text, rather than these aspects of a book's material presence.

Collections like EEBO and ECCO that strive to include an image for every work printed in a period present a different set of challenges.

Figure 38 Shown here are two views of the same page from a copy of John Donne's 1633 *Juvenilia*. On the left is that page as it is typically imaged. On the right is the same page shown with raking light, revealing that what appeared to be a blank, smooth surface is actually cockled and has blind type in the middle of the page reading "These eleuen Paradoxes, may bee printed." For more on this example, and for other considerations of a page's topography, see R. MacGeddon. Images made available by the Folger Shakespeare Library under a CC BY-SA 4.0 license (STC 7043.2, sig. F1v).

These databases are useful sources of digital images and easy to use in that you can readily search for a work and find a facsimile of it. They can also be misleading in their presentation of a copy as equivalent to a work. As we know, hand-press books are full of variants, from small stop-press changes to the insertion of cancel leaves. A single copy of an edition can easily differ from other copies in important ways. As one example, consider the 1791 edition of the poems of John Wilmot, Earl of Rochester (Wing R1756). Rochester's poems were scandalous for their sexually explicit content and their publication history is complex. In this posthumous edition, the editor and publisher Jacob Tonson replaced with a cancel a version of "Love a woman! You're an ass" that omits the song's final stanza, making it a slightly more decorous poem. The version on EEBO, however, is imaged from the Huntington Library's copy of the book, which has the original cancelland with the final lines, not the decorous cancel. Although the Huntington's catalog record notes that leaves D3 and D7 are cancellanda, there's nothing in EEBO's record pointing to this difference.

Although EEBO and ECCO present themselves as comprehensive databases of every work printed in English between 1473 and 1800, they are more accurately described as a collection of copies of works printed in those periods. If you are working with an image from those sources, you would be well served by always also looking at the ESTC record for the work, since variants are often recorded in their notes.

While it's easy to focus on the numerous things that digital facsimiles don't do, such images can also have an advantage over looking at a book in your hands. A book imaged at a high resolution can allow you to zoom in to see details in much greater focus than working with even a magnifying glass. Those details can help you see damaged type, the lines cut into a woodblock print, and the letters of tiny, cramped marginalia. Carefully imaged facsimiles can often compensate for bleed-through or poorly inked type by placing the leaf on top of a black sheet of paper or manipulating the contrast, making it easier to read than it would be in the reading room. And digital images can do even more complex work. Multispectral imaging can reveal features that are otherwise obscured; woodcuts used in different publications can quickly be matched across a large collection of material.

What's important to remember in working with digital facsimiles is that how they look is the result of choices made by the photographer and that those choices invariably mean that other ways of seeing the book are obscured. The images aren't neutral, in other words, but the result of a production process and institutional priorities.

Metadata

Just as books have catalog records detailing what they are, so should digital facsimiles. But while cataloging is a fairly standardized practice, the recording and sharing of equivalent information for digital facsimiles is not uniform. Libraries and commercial databases usually link their images to a catalog record. That should provide you with information about what you're looking at, but it can also be tricky. If what you're looking at is a few images from a book, rather than the entire book, the linked catalog record is likely to describe the book as a whole, rather than the images you're looking at; especially if the record includes copy-specific notes, those can be misleading when you're searching for something or trying to understand the characteristics of what you're seeing.

Another problem surfaces when using databases like EEBO and ECCO that have images from different libraries. Both provide catalog records that are drawn from the ESTC, which provides information about the edition, but not necessarily the copy shown. EEBO includes the name of the library holding the copy that was filmed (either in the "notes" section or as a separate field, depending on the interface you're using); it doesn't include a shelfmark, however, so if the institution has multiple copies, you'll still have a few more steps to go through to identify it. (In "Working with EEBO and ECCO" I describe how to identify imaged copies and provide other tips for using these databases; see Appendix 1.) Not all interfaces used to access ECCO, however, include the holding information for the copy imaged; those that do include only the library and not the shelfmark.

Greater problems abound in platforms that use automated systems to extract metadata from an item or that allow any user to create records. Google Books is notorious for misidentifying editions and volumes in a series. They can also misidentify the author and title. The British Library's copy of the 1668 edition of Margaret Cavendish's *Blazing World* (Wing N850) is in Google Books under the author "A. Maxwell," a mistake that probably comes from a catalog record that correctly identifies Maxwell as the publisher and doesn't list an author. The confusion is compounded by their use of the title of the work with which *Blazing World* was first published in 1666, *Observations upon experimental philosophy.* Facsimiles can also be listed as if they were the originals. Although Internet Archive's metadata suggests it includes a Hungarian New Testament first published in 1541 (USTC 305050), a closer look at the images themselves reveals that it's a facsimile printed in 1960.

Best practices for social media

Who can resist the urge to share pictures of a cool book? As long as you're allowed to, go ahead (but always check if you can take photos or if the photo you've found can be shared—more on licensing is below). If you do share an image, try to include in your post or tweet what it is and the library it's from. Sometimes you might have enough room to do that, but sometimes you might have to add that information in a comment or a linked tweet. Another option, one that can be especially useful for institutional social media, is to label the image itself with the library name and shelfmark (most image editors allow you to easily add text to an image).

Of course, the most frustrating images are those that circulate on social media platforms like Tumblr, Pinterest, and Twitter without any information about what is being shown, either for the work or for the holding institution. In those cases, the best you can do is to ask the original poster or to try a reverse image search to identify it.

Ideally, a digital facsimile should be accompanied not only by information about the object being depicted but by information about how the imaging was done. This would include information about the equipment used to take the image but also about the post-production processing, not to mention the date the image was taken. The most obvious example of the need for this are the digital collections which are made up entirely or largely of scans of microfilms, including EEBO, ECCO, and Gallica (the digital collection of the Bibliothèque nationale de France). In the case of EEBO, the dates when the films were made range from the 1940s up through today, but that information is not included in EEBO's scans, even though many of the microfilms include that data on target cards. For users encountering those databases for the first time, it's hard to understand why the images are in such a stark black and white without that contextual information.

Knowing whether an image has been treated after it was filmed can also convey important information about the relationship between what the screen is showing and what the object itself might look like. Is what is displayed as an image of a book opening actually two images of pages stitched together by post-processing software? If a book is bound tightly so that it only opens at 90° but the digital image of it shows it to be at 180°, the user of the digital image is missing information about the volume.

Imaging metadata might be displayed as part of a catalog record accompanying an image. But it can also appear as Exif or other data embedded in the image itself, so that if an image is downloaded, that information accompanies it and is displayed in the image viewer. More often than not, however, metadata about imaging is not provided. If it's important to your work, contacting the library that provided the image might help. (See the box "What is image metadata?" in Part 4 for more on metadata formats.)

What Can You Do with Digital Images?

One of the advantages of working with digital facsimiles is that they can be manipulated in ways that printed books cannot. Some of this seems obvious: if you are interested in a particular printer's device, for instance, you could collect title pages with the device separate from their books. If you have a question about a page feature, you can send a copy of an image to a colleague a few hundred miles away and get a second opinion. If you are giving a talk at a conference, you can include images comparing the 1610 Venice edition of Galileo's *Sidereus Nuncius* (USTC 4021754) with the pirated Frankfurt edition printed that same year (USTC 2067545).

What you can do with such images isn't limited by digital technology as much as it is by the parameters of the hosting platform and the terms under which they are made available for reuse.

Although popular culture often represents digital objects as unhampered by the material logistics of storage and production that paper books face, anything digital requires the same concerns about costs and maintenance. Many institutions have not provided public access to their highest resolution images out of concern for the file size and the bandwidth it takes to provide access. Hosting data costs money and the more data you want to serve up, the larger your servers need to be, and the larger the server, the higher the cost. As digital infrastructure costs come down, however, more institutions might provide greater access to digitizations.

But the biggest challenges in what you can do with digital images aren't technical hurdles but institutional permissions. Images are placed online with permitted uses ranging from none at all to personal use only to non-commercial use to public domain. Terms for reuse can be linked either to every image, to every book, or to the entire collection and can be written in easy-to-understand

Arguments for and against open access

Sometimes a library or archive is concerned that their images might be misidentified or misused if they allow them to circulate openly; sometimes they are driven by a belief that such images are a valuable source of income. But Michelle Light argues against that reasoning and for the importance of understanding open access as an imperative for special collections.

language or in dense legalese. Adding to the confusion is the range of legal opinions about whether faithful reproductions of public domain works can be copyrighted. Different jurisdictions are covered by different laws, and even where there are rulings that suggest reproductions of public domain works are themselves in the public domain, institutions often ignore those judgments and try to limit the possible uses of their image collections. In the United States, for example, the 1999 decision *Bridgman Art Library v Corel Corp.* held that exact photographic reproductions of public domain works could not be copyrighted since they lacked the necessary element of originality. But many US libraries and archives still assert copyright over their image collections and license their image only for certain uses.

By and large, you will encounter four levels of permissions when working with digital facsimiles of hand-press works. Some collections are completely restricted: you can look at the images online, but that's it. You can't share them in your teaching, you can't put them in presentations, you can't publish them in your book or on your website. This type of restriction was more common when libraries first started using digital images, and it is now on the wane.

Still in use is a slightly less restrictive licensing of images for personal use only or for personal use including research and teaching. In these cases, you can generally download the images when conducting your own research or for sharing with your students. You cannot, however, use them in publishing your research or distribute them beyond your classes. Different licenses might address whether conference presentations are a licensed usage, but often they leave that question silent.

The most common license you encounter in library digital collections is a non-commercial one, in which any usage is allowed as long as it is not for commercial purposes. In this case, you can use images in your research, in your classes, on your personal website (probably), and as part of your holiday cards. The line between commercial and non-commercial, however, is more blurred than you might think. Do you have ads on your website? Are you writing for a blog that's hosted by a newspaper or journal or press? Those are generally excluded from non-commercial uses.

Slowly gathering steam are "share-alike" licenses and public domain declarations, both of which allow the user great freedom in what can be done with images. For share-alike licenses, the general principle is that anything you create by altering the image must be licensed as share-alike or its equivalent. Want to create a print using images from a facsimile of Hobbes's *Leviathan*? As long as you sell your art under a share-alike license, you can do that. Need to reproduce a share-alike image in your book? That's generally fine. Public domain images allow you the greatest latitude: you can do anything you want.

To understand exactly what is and isn't allowed in using an image, carefully read the terms of use as stated on the collection's website. Sometimes an institution might use a license from Creative Commons or a statement from RightsStatements.org, both of which provide standardized and easy-to-understand terms. Regardless of how a license is stated, the responsibility is on you to understand what you are being given permission to do.

If you are reproducing a permitted image, even one in the public domain, it is best to treat it as you would any other object in need of citation, and to always cite both the work that is imaged and the holding institution along with it. Libraries invest money and effort in digitizing their collections and should be credited for their publication.

How Can You Find Digital Images?

The single biggest hurdle in working with digital facsimiles of hand-press books is finding them. If you have access to commercial databases like EEBO and ECCO, and the level of imaging and restricted permissions satisfies your needs, those are great places to start. (Even those can be hard to navigate, though. It's often easiest to start with ESTC records and follow their links to EEBO and ECCO.) But what if you aren't at an institution that provides access to those databases? (Neither allows for individual subscriptions and not all institutions can or choose to pay for them.) What if you're looking for works outside their remit? What if you need images that will let you reuse them on your website?

Although projects like the Digital Public Library of America (DPLA) and Europeana aim to create centralized access to digital images, they are still incomplete; not all libraries contribute their metadata to those hubs. ESTC and USTC provide other attempts at centralized listings of facsimiles, and they can be good places to start searching for hand-press books, especially since they have usually already vetted the metadata. Internet Archive and Google Books can also be good multi-source places to start searching, although the mess of incomplete and incorrect metadata can make it difficult. If you're looking for a specific work, one trick for proceeding is to look at union catalogs that identify holding institutions, and then try searching those libraries' digital collections.

Why is there so much digital Shakespeare?

There is little coordination among libraries in deciding what to digitize. Some places prioritize unique copies—books that don't exist anywhere else. Others create collections on a topic. But there are clear imbalances even within a field. At the moment of writing, there are 16 different copies of Shakespeare's First Folio that have been digitized. Other works central to the canon of English literature, however, don't exist in a single high-resolution copy: the first two editions of Sidney's *Astrophil and Stella* (STC 22536, 22637), any of the early editions of *Pilgrims Progress* (Wing B5557–B5579), or Aphra Behn's *Oronooko* (Wing B1749).

Sometimes you might be faced with the opposite problem: you'll come across an unidentified image of a book and want to find out more about it. Reverse image searching through TinEye or Google Image Search can sometimes help you trace back the image to its starting point. But image searches aren't always adept at differentiating between printed pages, and the original image doesn't always provide information. If you're looking at a full page, you might try to work out the book's title from the headline. Or if you're looking at an excerpt of a piece of text, you can try searching for an unusual phrase; if the book has been transcribed somewhere, or if that passage has been quoted, it might show up in searches.

With the expansion of USTC into the 17th century and with the addition of open-access digital copies to ESTC, it should become easier to find digital images of hand-press books. But for now, it takes perseverance and luck.

Conclusion

If we could pick up the book we considered in the introduction, the squat seven-language dictionary, it would look a lot more complex now, after having worked our way through this guide. You would recognize the broken remains of clasps for what they are; you might nod knowingly at the different typefaces used for the different languages; you could look at the addition of manuscript notes and understand how a user would expand into the endleaves to add her own vocabulary.

There are more questions we could ask, too, ones that might not have occurred to us before. You might have noticed on the title page that the imprint identifies this edition as being printed in Antwerp, and that matches what we see on the interior: Flemish is the first language listed and the English, frankly, is a bit wonky in its spelling and phrasing. But you might also have noticed that the book has an STC number, a catalog reference that usually is reserved for books printed in Britain. But remember the full title of the STC? It covers not only works printed in Britain and its colonies but works in English printed anywhere. And so this book, with one-seventh of its content in English, qualifies for inclusion in the STC. But why does the STC (and Wing, and the ESTC) include English-language books outside of Anglophone territories? Other national cataloging projects focus much more intensely on their geographic region. There was certainly a wide flow of movement in and out of England during the hand-press period as the Reformation waxed and waned and persecutions drove people out of the country. But other countries experienced similar patterns of emigration. What are the factors that drove the STC project to be shaped as it is?

We might also wonder why this popular genre of book—one that appears in a range of cataloging projects and that has survived in copies held in a multitude of libraries—is difficult to find online as a

Studying Early Printed Books 1450–1800: A Practical Guide, First Edition. Sarah Werner.
© 2019 Sarah Werner. Published 2019 by John Wiley & Sons Ltd.

Figure 39 The start of the Berlaimont text, with "Beloved reader" in seven languages and three typefaces, and some of the endleaves with a user's additional vocabulary notes. Images made available by the Folger Shakespeare Library under a CC BY-SA 4.0 license (STC 1431.86, sigs. A4v-A5r, 2D8v-facing endleaf; the last two have been digitally stitched together from two separate images).

high-resolution facsimile. The images that are reproduced in this book are the entirety of the images in Folger's digital collection not only of this copy, but of any of the 14 copies they hold. There are black-and-white images of microfilm in EEBO and Gallica (the digital library of the Bibliothèque nationale de France), and a few color copies from Madrid, Ghent, Tours, and Munich. But that's it. Why is this work, in any of its hundreds of editions, hardly worth imaging?

This edition of the Berlaimont offers some format questions as well: Is it an oblong 8mo or an oblong 16mo? Catalogers disagree, as is noted in its ESTC record. What would the implications of its production be for either choice?

Whether you can answer these questions or not was not the point of this book. Rather, what I hope you have learned is that there are questions to be asked when you see such a book, questions that you might not have known to ask before you started looking at it.

Books tell us stories. It's easy enough to read what's written. It's harder to read in a different type of language, to look at the signs left by long-ago workers about their unseen actions. But no book exists outside of its making, even the books you read today and scroll through on your phone. We can always ask: How was this made? What can knowing about its manufacture teach me about its audience and the story it's telling?

But we can't ask questions of objects we don't have. And libraries can only work as effectively as we let them. A student once told me that she felt sorry for the thousands and thousands of books closed away in the vault, never to be used by readers. How wonderful that they've been saved! But how lonely never to be read! At the time, I took it for granted that some books were read more often than others, that some texts were more desirable, some stories more urgent. But the longer I've worked with books, the more urgently I've felt her plea. We have lost unmeasurable numbers of texts over the centuries and we will never know what we're missing. But we have in front of us a treasure trove of information, from the most self-important to the most humble of books. They don't do anyone any good hidden away from readers who want to understand what they might tell us about their worlds. And we don't do future scholars any good by letting this cultural heritage slip through our fingers, locked away because it was too expensive to maintain or because we only valued what was utilitarian.

Go find the stories that these books tell us. And share them.

Appendix 1

Further Reading

This guide will get you started on exploring how early printed books were made and why it matters when we study them. But there's a world more of information out there on these questions. The readings listed below will get you started on exploring this field in greater depth. They are organized roughly by topic in the order they are addressed in the book, and with brief commentary. The exception to this organization are topics related to handling books, catalogs, and catalog resources—that is, things that I hope you will need as you use this guide hand in hand with reading early printed books.

For any topic related to the manufacture of hand-press books, the first place to start for more detail is Gaskell's *A New Introduction to Bibliography* (see below in general readings). A lengthier list of works is G. Thomas Tanselle's syllabus for his seminar "Introduction to Bibliography." The syllabus is available online through the University of Virginia's Rare Book School: http://rarebookschool. org/2011/tanselle/. Additional digital resources can be found at Early Printed Books (http://www.earlyprintedbooks.com).

General Bibliography

Bland, Mark. *A Guide to Early Printed Books and Manuscripts*. Chichester, UK: Wiley-Blackwell, 2010.
  A complement to Gaskell, with an additional focus on manuscripts and on how to use bibliography as an interpretive tool.

Blayney, Peter W. M. *The First Folio of Shakespeare*. Washington, DC: Folger Library Publications, 1991.
  A short pamphlet that, although focused on the First Folio, provides an accessible introduction to how books were printed and how bibliographical tools can be used to learn about their production.

Studying Early Printed Books 1450–1800: A Practical Guide, First Edition. Sarah Werner.
© 2019 Sarah Werner. Published 2019 by John Wiley & Sons Ltd.

Carter, John, Nicolas Barker, and Simran Thadani. *John Carter's ABC for Book Collectors*. 9th edition. New Castle, DE: Oak Knoll Press, 2016.
A handy glossary of terms used in talking about rare books. Also available in the 8th edition as a free pdf from the International League of Antiquarian Booksellers: https://ilab.org/articles/john-carter-abc-book-collectors.

Gaskell, Philip. *A New Introduction to Bibliography*. Reprinted with corrections in 1995. New Castle, DE: Oak Knoll Press, 2007.
The place to start for any further details; any questions you have about what you've learned here should drive you to Gaskell.

McKenzie, D. F. *Bibliography and the Sociology of Texts*. Cambridge: Cambridge University Press, 1999.
An influential and easy-to-read set of essays on the field of bibliography and its importance for scholarship.

Tanselle, G. Thomas. *Bibliographical Analysis: A Historical Introduction*. Cambridge: Cambridge University Press, 2009.
Very good for explaining why bibliographical analysis matters across general and specific topics; also has a useful bibliography.

Printer's Manuals

Moxon, Joseph. *Mechanick Exercises: or, the doctrine of handy-works. Applied to the art of Printing*. London: Joseph Moxon, 1683.
Volume 2 of a series about various skilled trades ("mechanical" here is used in its early sense of working at a trade with your hands). Also available (and preferable to read) in an Oxford edition edited by Harry Graham Carter and Herbert John Davis (2nd edition, 1962), which can also be found as a Dover reprint; a facsimile of the original is online from Boston Public Library: https://archive.org/details/mechanickexercis00moxo_0

Fertel, Martin-Dominique. *La Science Pratique de L'imprimerie*. Saint Omer: Martin Dominique Fertel, 1723.
A modern facsimile is available, but there are multiple ones online, including from Gallica: http://gallica.bnf.fr/ark:/12148/bpt6k1325424/

Encyclopédie ou Dictionnaire raisonné des sciences, des arts et des métiers, par une Société de Gens de lettres. Edited by Denis Diderot and Jean le Rond d'Alembert. Paris: Briasson, David, Le Breton, Durand, 1751–1772.
Multiple sections are devoted to hand-press related matters with some very useful illustrations. There's a Dover edition with facsimiles of the plates in two volumes (the section on "paper and printing" is in Volume 1) edited by Charles Gillespie (orig. 1959, reprint 1993). The transcribed text with facsimile plates is online from ARTFL Encyclopédie: http://

encyclopedie.uchicago.edu/; High-resolution facsimiles of the text and plates can be found at the Biodiversity Heritage Library: http://dx.doi. org/10.5962/bhl.title.77432

Smith, John. *The Printer's Grammar*. London: John Smith, 1755.
Focuses on compositors, not on presswork, but with additional information not in Moxon or Fertel; also available in an out-of-print facsimile from Gregg Press, but not online.

History of the Book

The history of the book is a broad field with many important contributions. The list below is just a smattering of works that are an easy introduction to the hand-press period or that I've referred to in this guide. Nationally focused series are also useful sources of information, including *The Cambridge History of The Book in Britain* (Cambridge University Press, 1999–), *The History of the Book in Canada* (University of Toronto Press, 2004–2007), *The History of the Book in America* (University of North Carolina Press, 2010), and *L'Histoire de l'édition française* (Promodis, 1983–1986).

Bruni, Flavia, and Andrew Pettegree, eds. *Lost Books: Reconstructing the Print World of Pre-Industrial Europe*. Leiden: Brill, 2016.
A collection of essays exploring what we know about books that haven't survived to today, how we can learn about them, and why it matters; Pettegree's introduction, "The Legion of the Lost: Recovering the Lost Books of Early Modern Europe," is an elucidating overview.

Buringh, Eltjo, and Jan Luiten Van Zanden. "Charting the 'Rise of the West': Manuscripts and Printed Books in Europe, A Long-Term Perspective from the Sixth through Eighteenth Centuries." *The Journal of Economic History* 69, 2 (2009): 409–445. doi:10.1017/S0022050709000837.
An economic perspective on how the development of print impacted Europe.

Eisenstein, Elizabeth L. *The Printing Revolution in Early Modern Europe*. 2nd edition, reprint. Canto Classics. Cambridge: Cambridge University Press, 2013.
The one-volume abridgment of Eisenstein's 1979 *The Printing Press as Agent of Change*, the influential work that in many ways kicked off the field of book history as we know it today. There has been, as with any foundational work, plenty of disagreement with it since its publication; see her exchange with Adrian Johns in the February 2002 issue of *American Historical Review* for one example.

Farmer, Alan B. "Playbooks and the Question of Ephemerality." In *The Book in History, the Book as History: New Intersections of the Material Text. Essays in Honor of David Scott Kastan*, edited by Heidi Brayman, Jesse M. Lander, and Zachary Lesser, 87–125. New Haven, CT: Yale University Press, 2016.

A methodologically careful and clear explanation of calculating loss rates and then extrapolating from that to what can be described as ephemeral or popular.

Harris, Neil. "The Italian Book: Catalogue, Censuses and Survival." In *The Book Triumphant: Print in Transition in the Sixteenth and Seventeenth Centuries*, edited by Malcolm Walsby and Graeme Kemp, 26–56. Leiden: Brill, 2011.
 Uses statistical methods to explore the number of Italian books that have not survived and what that means.

Pettegree, Andrew. *The Book in the Renaissance*. New Haven: Yale University Press, 2010.
 An accessible and enjoyable read about the printed book in Renaissance Europe.

Book Trade

Blayney, Peter W. M. "The Publication of Playbooks." In *A New History of Early English Drama*, edited by John D. Cox and David Scott Kastan, 383–422. New York: Columbia University Press, 1997.
 Read for the account of the different roles of stationers and the process of printing a book and as a good introduction to the purpose and practices of the Stationers' Company.

Davis, Natalie Zemon. "Women in the Crafts in Sixteenth-Century Lyon." *Feminist Studies* 8, 1 (1982): 46. doi:10.2307/3177579.
 About artisans in general, but includes a look at printers and is a good framework for thinking about women's connections to labor in this period.

Parker, Deborah. "Women in the Book Trade in Italy, 1475–1620." *Renaissance Quarterly* 49, 3 (1996): 509–541. doi:10.2307/2863365.
 A look at and argument for the importance of studying women printers.

Raven, James. *The Business of Books: Booksellers and the English Book Trade 1450–1850*. New Haven, CT: Yale University Press, 2007.
 A good place to start exploring the economic dynamics of the English book trade.

Remer, Rosalind. *Printers and Men of Capital: Philadelphia Book Publishers in the New Republic*. Philadelphia: University of Pennsylvania Press, 1996.
 The shift from printing to building an American book trade.

Smith, Helen. *"Grossly Material Things": Women and Book Production in Early Modern England*. Oxford: Oxford University Press, 2012.
 The place to start for learning about women in the English book trade.

Stallybrass, Peter. "'Little Jobs': Broadsides and the Printing Revolution." In *Agent of Change: Print Culture Studies After Elizabeth L. Eisenstein*, edited by Sabrina A. Baron, Eric N. Lindquist, and Eleanor F. Shevlin, 315–341. Amherst: University of Massachusetts Press, 2007.

The centrality of broadsides to understanding how print shops stayed afloat and what their production can tell us about the book trade.

Voet, Leon. *The Golden Compasses: A History and Evaluation of the Printing and Publishing Activities of the Officina Plantiniana at Antwerp.* Amsterdam: Vangendt, 1969.
The detailed account of the Plantin-Moretus printing house, drawing on their long-kept archives; also available at http://www.dbnl.org/tekst/voet004gold01_01/index.php

Manuscripts and Paleography

McKitterick, David. *Print, Manuscript, and the Search for Order, 1450–1830.* Cambridge: Cambridge University Press, 2003.
An engaging account of interplay between print and manuscript.

Penn in Hand: Selected Manuscripts. University of Pennsylvania. http://dla.library.upenn.edu/dla/medren/index.html
Digitized medieval and Renaissance manuscripts.

EMMO: Early Modern Manuscripts Online. Folger Shakespeare Library. http://emmo.folger.edu/
Images of early modern English manuscripts along with transcriptions.

"List of Online Resources for Early Modern English paleography." *Folgerpedia.* Folger Shakespeare Library. http://folgerpedia.folger.edu/List_of_online_resources_for_early_modern_English_paleography
Resources for learning how to read early handwriting and a list of online repositories of early modern manuscripts.

"Secretary Hand Alphabet." *Rediscovering Rycote: The Lost History of a Tudor Mansion.* Bodleian Libraries. http://rycote.bodleian.ox.ac.uk/Palaeography-Guide-alphabet
Includes dated examples of different letters and abbreviations as written in secretary hand; for specimens see also Gaskell.

Handling Books

Baker, Cathleen A., and Randy Silverman. "Misperceptions about White Gloves." *International Preservation News* 37 (2005): 4–9.
A thorough look at why wearing white gloves can actually increase potential damage when handling rare books.

Folger Shakespeare Library. Handling Rare Materials, 2011. https://www.youtube.com/watch?v=5NWyruNYILw

An introduction to how to handle rare books, manuscripts, and other items, demonstrating using cradles, book weights, and phase boxes.

Catalogs of Early Hand-press Books

A partial list of union catalogs of hand-press books, organized alphabetically. Most of these are online and many have English interfaces as an option.

EDIT16 (Censimento nazionale delle edizioni italiane del XVI secolo): http://edit16.iccu.sbn.it/web_iccu/ihome.htm
A catalog of editions printed in Italy or in Italian in the 16th century; includes information about printers' devices, dedications, images related to bibliographic information, devices, or dedications, Italian holdings information, and links to digitizations; uses LOC fingerprints.

ESTC (English Short Title Catalogue): http://estc.bl.uk
A catalog of items published between 1473 and 1800 that are in English or that were printed in the British Isles or British colonies; includes holdings information and links to digitizations, primarily to EEBO and ECCO, but with open-access images being added. The ESTC incorporates earlier catalogs— STC, Wing, the Eighteenth Century Short Title Catalogue, and Evans—and so is not always consistent on what types of items are included or what information is recorded. The STC included ephemera and periodicals, for example, while Wing did not include either, but Evans did record periodicals.

Evans (*American Bibliography: A Chronological Dictionary of All Books, Pamphlets, and Periodical Publications Printed in the United States of America from the Genesis of Printing in 1639 down to and Including the Year 1820*, edited by Charles Evans. Reprint. New York: P. Smith, 1941–1959.)
A print catalog of American imprints up to 1820; the entire collection (aside from serials) was microfilmed and is now available as a commercial digital database called *Early American Imprints*; a facsimile of the catalog, including the index that comprises the 14th volume, is available at HathiTrust: https://catalog.hathitrust.org/Record/001167956. Items in Evans are now part of the online ESTC.

GW (Gesamtkatalog der Wiegendrucke): http://www.gesamtkatalogder wiegendrucke.de/
A descriptive catalog of editions printed before 1501; includes bibliographic details, holdings information, and links to digitizations. The catalog is an extension of the earlier print volumes, and the amount of detail included depends on whether the record is adapted from the detailed print publication or it is a temporary entry awaiting further research; information about what is included for which records is in the catalog's introduction.

ISTC (Incunabula Short Title Catalogue): http://data.cerl.org/istc/
A catalog of nearly all editions printed before 1501; includes holding information and links to digitizations. On the one hand, the information here is much less detailed than in GW; on the other, the ISTC is easier to search and provides links to GW and other incunable catalogs.

STC (Short-Title Catalogue; *A Short-Title Catalogue of Books Printed in England, Scotland, & Ireland and of English Books Printed Abroad, 1475–1640*, edited by Alfred W. Pollard, G. R. Redgrave, William A. Jackson, F. S. Ferguson, and Katharine F. Pantzer. 2nd edition, revised and enlarged. London: Bibliographical Society, 1976.)
A print-only catalog, now incorporated into the online ESTC, but still useful on its own. STC numbers continue to be a standard reference point, and entries often include information that hasn't been incorporated into ESTC. Volume 3 has indices that are essential for research in this period. The 2nd edition of the STC, listed here, is substantially revised from the first; many numbers changed, so it's always best to use this edition.

STCN (Short-Title Catalog, Netherlands): http://www.stcn.nl
A catalog of editions published in the Netherlands or in Dutch between 1540 and 1800; editions are cataloged book-in-hand (that is, by looking at specific copies rather than adopting catalog records from other sources); includes typographical information and links to digitizations; does not include broadsheets or periodicals; uses STCN fingerprints.

STCV (Short Title Catalogus Vlaanderen): http://www.stcv.be/en
A catalog of editions published in Flanders before 1801; editions are cataloged book-in-hand (that is, by looking at specific copies rather than adopting catalog records from other sources); includes typographical information, descriptions of paratexts, images of key bibliographic pages, and links to digitizations; broadsides were initially excluded and are now being added in; periodicals not included; uses STCN fingerprints.

USTC (Universal Short Title Catalogue): http://ustc.ac.uk/
An in-progress catalog of all books published in Europe up to 1600, with records up to 1650 currently being added; includes holdings information and links to digitizations. The USTC incorporates entries within its time period of coverage from most of the catalogs listed here, and includes fingerprints if they are in the source data.

VD16 (Verzeichnis der im deutschen Sprachbereich erschienenen Drucke des XVI. Jahrhunderts): http://www.vd16.de/
A union catalog of works published in German-language regions in the 16th century; doesn't include broadsheets; includes German holdings information and links to digitizations.

VD17 (Das Verzeichnis der im deutschen Sprachraum erschienenen Drucke des 17. Jahrhunderts): http://www.vd17.de/
A union catalog of works published in German-language regions or in German in adjacent regions in the 17th century; includes links to digitizations and images of "key pages," usually title page, names of dedicatees, first page of the main text, and colophon; uses LOC fingerprints.

VD18 (Digitalisierung und Erschließung der im deutschen Sprachraum erschienenen Drucke des 18. Jahrhunderts): http://www.vd18.de/
An in-progress union catalog and digitization of works published in German-language regions in the 18th century.

Wing (*Short-Title Catalogue of Books Printed in England, Scotland, Ireland, Wales, and British America, and of English Books Printed in Other Countries, 1641–1700*, edited by Donald Goddard Wing and Modern Language Association of America. 2nd edition, newly revised and enlarged. New York: Index Committee of the Modern Language Association of America, 1982.)
A print-only catalog that is now incorporated into the online ESTC, but is still a standard reference point and a useful source; doesn't include ephemera or periodicals. This revised edition is significantly more accurate, and updated, from the first edition.

Catalog and Imprint Resources

CERL Thesaurus. Consortium of European Research Libraries. http://thesaurus.cerl.org/
A database of imprint places, imprint names, personal names, and corporate names, including variant spellings, forms in Latin and other languages, and fictitious names.

Cheney, C. R. ed. *A Handbook of Dates: For Students of British History*. New edition, revised by Michael Jones. Cambridge: Cambridge University Press, 2000.
As many details as you could possibly want, including charts of reigns and holidays, for understanding early modern British dates.

Fingerprints, Empreintes, Impronte. Institut de Recherche et d'Histoire des Textes. 1984. http://edit16.iccu.sbn.it/web_iccu/info/en/Impronta.htm
The manual, with examples, for the LOC fingerprinting methodology.

Harris, Neil. "Tribal Lays and the History of the Fingerprint." In *Many into One: Problems and Opportunities in Creating Shared Catalogues of Older Books*, edited by David J. Shaw, 21–72. London: Consortium of European Research Libraries, 2006.

An explanation and examination of various systems of bibliographic fingerprinting; also at http://people.uniud.it/node/781

RBMS/BSC Latin Place Names File. Rare Books and Manuscript Section. Created and maintained by Robert L. Maxwell, Harold B. Lee Library, Brigham Young University. https://rbms.info/lpn/
A searchable list of locations found in early modern texts and their Latin and vernacular names. Also helpful is this glossary of common Latin terms found in imprint statements: https://rbms.info/lpn/glossary-of-common-latin-terms-found-in-imprints-of-early-printed-books/

RBMS/BSC Standard Citation Forms for Rare Materials Cataloging. Rare Books and Manuscript Section. https://rbms.info/scf/
A database providing full citations for references found in catalogs, searchable by shortened form.

Vriesema, P. C. A. "The STCN Fingerprint." *Studies in Bibliography* 39 (1986): 93–100. http://www.jstor.org/stable/40371834
Explains the STCN fingerprint methodology; see also Goran Proot's posts for the Folger's *Collation* for a clear and illustrated account of how it works and its uses: http://collation.folger.edu/2012/09/detective-work-the-dutch-fingerprint-part-i/ and http://collation.folger.edu/2012/10/second-thoughts-on-second-editions-the-dutch-fingerprint-part-ii/

Paper

Barrett, Timothy. "European Papermaking Techniques 1300–1800." *Paper through Time: Nondestructive Analysis of 14th- through 19th-Century Papers*. University of Iowa. http://paper.lib.uiowa.edu/european.php
The place to start with questions about how paper was made in the period, albeit very detailed; also worth watching the video of Barrett and his students making paper: https://www.youtube.com/watch?v=e-PmfdV_cZU

Bidwell, John. "The Study of Paper as Evidence, Artefact, and Commodity." In *The Book Encompassed: Studies in Twentieth-Century Bibliography*, edited by Peter Hobley Davison. New Castle, DE: Oak Knoll Press, 1998.
An accessible overview of why studying paper matters; excerpt available from International League of Antiquarian Booksellers: https://www.ilab.org/articles/study-paper-evidence-artefact-and-commodity

Bidwell, John. "French Paper in English Books." In *The Cambridge History of the Book in Britain. Volume 4: 1557–1695*, edited by John Barnard and D. F. McKenzie, Reprint, 583–601. Cambridge: Cambridge University Press, 2009.
A good overview of the paper trade.

Hunter, Dard. *Papermaking: The History and Technique of an Ancient Craft.*
2nd revised edition. New York: A. A. Knopf, 1947.
The standard reference on papermaking techniques; also available in a
Dover reprint.

Stevenson, Allan. "Paper as Bibliographical Evidence." *The Library* series 5,
vol. 17, 3 (1962): 197–212. doi:10.1093/library/s5-XVII.3.197.
A clear and enjoyable account of the ways in which paper can reveal
bibliographical evidence, with an examination of the paper in the *Missale
speciale* as a method of dating.

Vander Meulen, David. "The Identification of Paper without Watermarks:
The Example of Pope's 'Dunciad.'" *Studies in Bibliography* 37 (1984): 58–81.
http://www.jstor.org/stable/40371793
A good description of what characteristic papermarks are aside from
watermarks, with detailed methodology and illustrated with an
examination of the paper in Pope's "Dunciad."

Type

Agüera y Arcas, Blaise. "Temporary Matrices and Elemental Punches in
Gutenberg's DK Type." In *Incunabula and Their Readers: Printing, Selling
and Using Books in the Fifteenth Century,* edited by Kristian Jensen, 1–12.
London: British Library, 2003.
A careful study arguing that Gutenberg made his early type with sand casting.

Carter, Harry. *A View of Early Typography up to About 1600.* Reprint of
1969 with new introduction by James Mosley. London: Hyphen, 2002.
A detailed account of early typemaking and typography; the place to start
for more information.

Chappell, Warren, and Robert Bringhurst, *A Short History of the Printed
Word.* 2nd edition. Vancouver: Hartley & Marks, 1999.
An accessibly written and nicely illustrated introduction to everything
related to "the printed word" including typography.

Hinman, Charlton. *The Printing and Proofreading of Shakespeare's First Folio.*
Oxford: Clarendon Press, 1963.
Not for beginners, but a magisterial account of how the First Folio was
printed, based on careful collation of 53 copies of the book; the foundation
for later studies not only of F1 but of using type to recreate printing history.

Lesser, Zachary. "Typographic Nostalgia: Playreading, Popularity, and Black
Letter." In *The Book of the Play: Playwrights, Stationers, and Readers in
Early Modern England,* edited by Marta Straznicky, 99–126. Amherst:
University of Massachusetts Press, 2006.

An argument for seeing some uses of black letter in English printing as a deliberate choice to evoke a nostalgia for the past.

Reske, Christoph. "Hat Johannes Gutenberg Das Gießinstrument Erfunden? Mikroskopischer Typenvergleich an Frühen Drucken." *Gutenberg Jahrbuch* 90 (2015): 44–63.
A reconsideration and rebuttal of Agüera y Arcas's argument that Gutenberg used temporary molds to cast his type.

Weiss, Adrian. "Font Analysis as a Bibliographical Method: The Elizabethan Play-Quarto Printers and Compositors." *Studies in Bibliography* 43 (1990): 95–164. http://www.jstor.org/stable/40371924
A good explanation and illustration of how font analysis can help identify printers.

Format

For more details about and diagrams of different impositions, see Gaskell and the printer's manuals.

Dane, Joseph, and Alexandra Gillespie. "The Myth of the Cheap Quarto." In *Tudor Books and Readers: Materiality and the Construction of Meaning*, edited by John N. King, 25–45. Cambridge: Cambridge University Press, 2010.
Questioning received wisdom about what signals are sent by a work being printed in quarto.

Galbraith, Steven Kenneth. "English Literary Folios." In *Tudor Books and Readers: Materiality and the Construction of Meaning*, edited by John N. King, 46–65. Cambridge: Cambridge University Press, 2010.
Rethinking why and how decisions were made to print works in folio.

Tanselle, G. Thomas. "The Concept of Format." *Studies in Bibliography* 53 (2000): 67–115. doi:10.2307/40372094.
Defining format—it's more complicated and important than you first think.

Printing

Cloud, Random [Randall McLeod]. "Where Angels Fear to read." In *Ma(r)king the Text*, edited by Joe Bray, Miriam Handley, and Anne C. Henry, 144–192. Aldershot: Ashgate, 2000.
Uses bearing text to track concurrent printing.

MacGeddon, R. [Randall McLeod]. "Hammered." In *Negotiating the Jacobean Printed Book*, edited by Pete Langman, 137–199. Farnham, UK: Ashgate, 2011.

A typically engaging look from McLeod at unexpected bibliographic details, here primarily focused on the textures of the printed page left by blind type and binders' hammers.

McKenzie, D. F. "Printers of the Mind: Some Notes on Bibliographical Theories and Printing-House Practices." *Studies in Bibliography* 22 (1969): 1–75. http://www.jstor.org/stable/40371475
A foundational study reassessing common assumptions about how printing practices worked.

Nelson, Stan, and Peter Herdrich. *From Punch to Printing Type: The Art & Craft of Hand Punchcutting and Typecasting*. Videorecording. Book Arts Press, 1985.
An easy-to-watch 57-minute recording of Stan Nelson making a piece of type from scratch; a series of films featuring Nelson covering the same subjects are on YouTube: https://www.youtube.com/playlist?list=PLD1C9 18AD04AF88E0

Tanselle, G. Thomas. "The Treatment of Typesetting and Presswork in Bibliographical Description." *Studies in Bibliography* 52 (1999): 1–57. http://www.jstor.org/stable/40372076
Although the focus is on how typesetting and presswork should be incorporated into bibliographic descriptions, the article includes overviews of why such information is valuable.

Weiss, Adrian. "A 'Fill-In' Job: The Textual Crux and Interrupted Printing in Thomas Middleton's 'The Triumphs of Honor and Virtue' (1622)." *The Papers of the Bibliographical Society of America* 93, 1 (1999): 53–73. http://www.jstor.org/stable/24304373
Uses the bibliographic evidence of presswork to determine how the printer scheduled work in his shop.

Corrections

Blair, Ann. "Errata Lists and the Reader as Corrector." In *Agent of Change: Print Culture Studies after Elizabeth L. Eisenstein*, edited by Sabrina A. Baron, Eric N. Lindquist, and Eleanor F. Shevlin, 21–41. Amherst: University of Massachusetts Press, 2007.
An account of how readers responded (and didn't) to errata lists.

Dane, Joseph A., and Seth Lerer. "Press Variants in John Stow's Chaucer (1561) and the Text of 'Adam Scriveyn.'" *Transactions of the Cambridge Bibliographical Society* 11, 4 (1999): 468–479. http://www.jstor.org/stable/41154884.
A look at the complexity of changes made in the two states of this book and how they came about.

Grafton, Anthony. *The Culture of Correction in Renaissance Europe.*
London: British Library, 2011.
   A look at how authors and print shops dealt with wanting and making
   corrections, with lots of examples and illustrations.

Kelemen, Erick, ed. *Textual Editing and Criticism: An Introduction.* New
York: W.W. Norton, 2009.
   A straightforward introduction to editing and the types of choices and
   uses of evidence to make decisions.

Simpson, Percy. *Proof-Reading in the Sixteenth, Seventeenth and Eighteenth
Centuries.* London: Oxford University Press, H. Milford, 1935.
   The foundational study on the subject, though not without errors,
   including an assumption that authors routinely read proofs.

Wood, E. R. "Cancels and Corrections in *A Discovering of Errors*, 1622." *The
Library* series 5, vol. 13, 2 (1958): 124–127. doi:10.1093/library/s5-XIII.2.124.
   A list of the different types and locations of corrections in Vincent's book.
   There is a digital facsimile of the Getty Research Institute's copy of the
   book online at Internet Archive that contains most of these corrections:
   https://archive.org/details/discouerieoferro00vinc

Illustrations

Blake, Erin. "Woodcut, Engraving, or What"? *The Collation.* Folger
Shakespeare Library. February 7, 2012. http://collation.folger.edu/2012/02/
woodcut-engraving-or-what/
   A good introduction to identifying woodcuts, engravings, and etchings,
   with detailed images.

Gascoigne, Bamber. *How to Identify Prints: A Complete Guide to Manual
and Mechanical Processes from Woodcut to Inkjet.* 2nd edition. New York:
Thames & Hudson, 2004.
   Particularly useful for learning how to tell the difference between
   different techniques, with helpful illustrations.

Gaskell, Roger. "Printing House and Engraving Shop. A Mysterious
Collaboration." *The Book Collector* 53 (2004): 213–251.
   A look at how engravings worked as book illustrations in terms of production
   and the book trade; also available at http://www.rogergaskell.com/
   custom?page=14

Griffiths, Antony. *Prints and Printmaking: An Introduction to the History
and Techniques.* Berkeley: University of California Press, 1996.
   The place to start to learn about various printing techniques; the focus is
   on prints, not book illustrations, but the technologies are largely the same.

Hedges, Blair. "A Method for Dating Early Books and Prints Using Image Analysis." *Proceedings of the Royal Society A: Mathematical, Physical and Engineering Sciences* 462, 2076 (2006): 3555–3573. doi:10.1098/rspa.2006.1736.

Hedges, Blair. "Image Analysis of Renaissance Copperplate Prints." *Proceedings of SPIE* 6810 (2008): 681009.
> Together, these articles provide a technical account of using image analysis to determine the rate of wear and lifespan of woodblocks and copperplates and how that information can be used to date works. A more general-reader-friendly account of this process, with helpful images, can be found at Hedges's site, *The Print Clock*: http://www.printclock.org/

Luborsky, Ruth Samson, and Elizabeth Morley Ingram. *A Guide to English Illustrated Books, 1536–1603*. Tempe, AZ: Medieval & Renaissance Texts & Studies, 1998.
> A useful (and unique) catalog of illustrations and their reuse across different books; helpful in tracing the history of woodblock usage as well as in looking at the iconography of the period.

Bindings

Foot, Mirjam M. *The History of Bookbinding as a Mirror of Society*. London: British Library, 1998.
> An argument for the ways in which studying bindings contributes to understanding the history of books and of culture.

Knight, Jeffrey Todd. *Bound to Read: Compilations, Collections, and the Making of Renaissance Literature*. Philadelphia: University of Pennsylvania Press, 2013.
> How Renaissance books have been bound, unbound, and rebound over the centuries to make them conform to our sense of what literature is.

Pearson, David. *English Bookbinding Styles, 1450–1800: A Handbook*. London: British Library, 2005.
> The place to begin studying more about bookbindings in this period; the focus is on English bindings, but the book is also useful for general information.

Pearson, David, John Mumford, and Alison Walker. *Bookbindings*. Preservation Advisory Centre. Revised. London: British Library, 2010.
> A clear introduction to bindings, written with an eye to how to preserve them, but a useful brief on their structures and history. Available online at http://www.bl.uk/aboutus/stratpolprog/collectioncare/publications/booklets/caring_for_bookbindings.pdf

Pratt, Aaron T. "Stab-Stitching and the Status of Early English Playbooks as Literature." *The Library* 16, 3 (2015): 304–328. doi:10.1093/library/16.3.304.
Argues for rethinking the prevalence of stab-stitching and what it signifies about the work so bound.

On the Page

See also "Catalog and Imprint Resources" earlier in this appendix for additional resources.

Advertisements

Hooks, Adam G. "Booksellers' Catalogues and the Classification of Printed Drama in Seventeenth-Century England." *The Papers of the Bibliographical Society of America* 102, 4 (2008): 445–464. doi:10.1086/pbsa.102.4.24293688.
Uses the categorization of drama in booksellers' lists to argue for a codification of dramatic genres and to trace the inventory of booksellers.

Collation Formulas

Bowers, Fredson. *Principles of Bibliographical Description*. Princeton: Princeton University Press, 1949.
Primarily of use for those wanting to learn bibliographic description, but as such includes definitive explanations of the elements of collational formulas as well as of what issues and states are; also available in a 1994 reprint with an introduction by Tanselle.

Edition, Impression, Issue, State

Tanselle, G. Thomas. "The Bibliographical Concepts of 'Issue' and 'State.'" *The Papers of the Bibliographical Society of America* 69, 1 (1975): 17–66. http://www.jstor.org/stable/24302244
With Bowers, a useful guide to the differences between "issue" and "state."

Press Figures

Dawson, Robert. "Notes on Press-Figures in France and the Localization of Books during the Later 18th Century." *Bulletin of the Bibliographical Society of Australia and New Zealand* 28, 3 (2004): 97–121.
On how to differentiate the rare use of press figures outside of Britain from false imprints; available online at http://www.bsanz.org/download/bulletin-/bulletin_vol._28_no._3_(2004)/B_2004_Vol28_No3_06.pdf

Todd, William B. "Observations on the Incidence and Interpretation of Press Figures." *Studies in Bibliography* 3 (1950): 171–205. http://www.jstor. org/stable/40381882
Foundational study of where press figures occur and what they might mean.

Printer's Devices

McKerrow, R. B. *Printer's & Publishers' Devices in England & Scotland, 1485–1640.* London: Bibliographical Society, 1913.
An illustrated account of devices; still available in reprints, but a facsimile of the 1st edition can be found at the Internet Archive: http://archive.org/ details/b24749722

Printer's Ornaments

Fleming, Juliet. "How to Look at a Printed Flower." *Word & Image* 22, 2 (2006): 165–187. doi:10.1080/02666286.2006.10435743.

Fleming, Juliet. "How Not to Look at a Printed Flower." *Journal of Medieval and Early Modern Studies* 38, 2 (2008): 345–371. doi:10.1215/10829636-2007-029.

Fleming, Juliet. "Changed Opinion As To Flowers." In *Renaissance Paratexts*, edited by Helen Smith and Louise Wilson, 34–64. Cambridge: Cambridge University Press, 2008.
Together, an important series on the little-studied bibliographic and rhetorical uses of printers' flowers.

Signature Marks

Sayce, R. A. "Compositorial Practices and the Localization of Printed Books 1530–1800." *The Library* series 5, vol. 21, 1 (1966), 1–45. Reprinted, with corrections and additions, by the Oxford Bibliographical Society, Oxford, 1977.
An important and exhaustive study of how signature marks, dating, and other practices varied from location to location.

Title Pages

Smith, Margaret M. *The Title-Page: Its Early Development, 1460–1510.* London: British Library, 2000.
The primary study of early title pages, clearly written and illustrated.

Volvelles

Drennan, Anthony S. "The Bibliographical Description of Astronomical Volvelles and Other Moveable Diagrams." *The Library* 13, 3 (2012): 316–339. doi:10.1093/library/13.3.316.
An exploration of how to indicate the presence of volvelles in bibliographic descriptions, but also includes accounts of their different constructions.

Karr, Suzanne. "Constructions Both Sacred and Profane: Serpents, Angels, and Pointing Fingers in Renaissance Books with Moving Parts." *The Yale University Library Gazette* 78, 3/4 (2004): 101–127. http://www.jstor.org/stable/40859568
A look at the range of uses for movable books, by way of some specific examples.

Afterlives

Works about survival rates are included in the earlier "History of the Book" section; paleographic resources can be found in the earlier "Manuscripts and Paleography" section.

Exhumation [Ian Jackson]. *Chamberpot and Motherfuck: The Price-Codes of the Book-Trade.* 2nd edition, revised and enlarged. Narberth, PA: Bruce McKittrick, 2017.
The primary source of information about how price codes work, as well as a list of examples.

Fumerton, Patricia, Carl G. Stahmer, Kris McAbee, and Megan Palmer Brown. "Vexed Impressions: Towards a Digital Archive of Broadside Ballad Illustrations." In *Digitizing Medieval and Early Modern Material Culture*, edited by Brent Nelson and Melissa M. Terras, 259–287. Tempe, AZ: Arizona Center for Medieval and Renaissance Studies, 2012.
A detailed look at the considerations about what and how to digitize broadsides, from the creators of the English Broadside Ballad Archive.

Giacometti, Alejandro, Alberto Campagnolo, Lindsay MacDonald, Simon Mahony, Stuart Robson, Tim Weyrich, Melissa Terras, and Adam Gibson. "The Value of Critical Destruction: Evaluating Multispectral Image Processing Methods for the Analysis of Primary Historical Texts." *Digital Scholarship in the Humanities*, 32, 1 (2017): 101–122. doi:10.1093/llc/fqv036.
A consideration of how well multispectral imaging works to recover texts from damaged documents.

Light, Michelle. "Controlling Goods or Promoting the Public Good: Choices for Special Collections in the Marketplace." *RBM: A Journal of Rare Books, Manuscripts and Cultural Heritage* 16, 1 (2015): 48–63. doi:10.5860/rbm.16.1.435.
A persuasive argument from a special collections librarian that libraries are ethically compelled to open up their digital collections for the public good.

Mak, Bonnie. "Archaeology of a Digitization." *Journal of the Association for Information Science and Technology* 65, 8 (2014): 1515–1526. doi:10.1002/asi.23061.
A consideration of EEBO through the lens of its layered history of media.

McKitterick, David. *Old Books, New Technologies: The Representation, Conservation and Transformation of Books Since 1700*. Cambridge: Cambridge University Press, 2013.
A thoughtful look at how old books have been treated since the early modern period.

Pearson, David. *Provenance Research in Book History: A Handbook*. London: British Library & Oak Knoll Press, 1994.
An essential guidebook for studying previous owners of a book.

Sherman, William H. *Used Books: Marking Readers in Renaissance England*. Philadelphia: University of Pennsylvania Press, 2007.
Focuses primarily on the sorts of marks that early modern English readers left in their books, but also considers the role that collectors have had in preserving (or not) those marks.

Strlič, Matija, Jacob Thomas, Tanja Trafela, Linda Cséfalvayová, Irena Kralj Cigić, Jana Kolar, and May Cassar. "Material Degradomics: On the Smell of Old Books." *Analytical Chemistry* 81, 20 (2009): 8617–8622. doi:10.1021/ac9016049.
A chemical study examining the elements that make up characteristic smells of old books and proposing their value as a diagnostic tool for conservation.

Werner, Sarah. "Digital First Folios." In *The Cambridge Companion to Shakespeare's First Folio*, edited by Emma Smith, 170–184. Cambridge: Cambridge University Press, 2016.
Models an examination of digital facsimiles in terms of access, bibliography, and cultural materialism; also available at http://sarahwerner.net/blog/wp-content/uploads/2017/02/Werner_digital-F1s_website.pdf

Werner, Sarah. "Working with EEBO and ECCO." 2017. doi:dx.doi.org/10.17613/M6J96G.
A guide to using EEBO and ECCO, including searching, thinking through their media history, and connecting them to other catalogs.

Digital Collections

I maintain a longer list of share-alike or public domain digital collections of early modern books at Early Printed Books (http://www.earlyprintedbooks.com).

DPLA (Digital Public Library of America): http://dp.la
   An open-access portal to digital collections of libraries and archives across America.

EBBA (English Broadside Ballad Archive): https://ebba.english.ucsb.edu/
   An openly accessible database of nearly 8,000 English ballads from the 17th century; includes facsimile images as well as transcriptions and recordings of melodies.

ECCO (Eighteenth Century Collections Online): http://www.gale.com/primary-sources/eighteenth-century-collections-online/
   A Gale subscription database of digital scans of microfilms of books printed in the United Kingdom between 1701 and 1800.

EEB (Early European Books): http://proquest.libguides.com/eeb
   A ProQuest subscription database of digital images of books printed in continental Europe up until 1700.

EEBO (Early English Books Online): http://proquest.libguides.com/eebo
   A ProQuest subscription database of digital scans of microfilms of books printed in English or in the British Isles and colonies between 1475 and 1700.

Europeana: http://www.europeana.eu/portal/en
   An open-access portal to digital collections of libraries and museums across Europe.

Gallica: http://gallica.bnf.fr
   The open-access digital collection of the Bibliothèque nationale de France.

Appendix 2

Glossary

Bearing type Uninked type used to even out the printing surface when parts of a page are intended to be left empty; sometimes called "bearer's type" or "blind type."

Bibliography A capacious term which I narrow in this guide to the study of how books are made; in other uses it can mean a list of books or a description of books.

Boards Technically, the hard material used in bindings, which then may be covered in leather or other materials. But the term is also used more generally to refer to the boards and their coverings, as in "the upper board is loose, so handle it carefully."

Bookseller A person whose primary function was to sell books either to the public (retail) or to other members of the printers' guild (usually wholesale). A bookseller might also function at times as a publisher.

Broadside, broadsheet (1°) A sheet that has been printed as a single leaf, rather than folded into smaller leaves. The term is often used to describe any sheet that has been printed on a single side, regardless of format (e.g. a ballad printed on half a sheet of paper); it has also come to be used as a genre term for proclamations and ballads and other works that were printed in this format.

Cancel The part of a book that corrects and replaces the original printed text; it might be as small as a slip pasted over a word, or it might be multiple leaves sewn into the gathering. The original text or leaf that will be replaced is called a cancelland (or cancellandum); the replacement is the cancel (or cancellans).

Casting off The process of determining how much text goes on each printed page; the compositor reads through the copy text to cast it off and marks it up accordingly.

Studying Early Printed Books 1450–1800: A Practical Guide, First Edition. Sarah Werner.
© 2019 Sarah Werner. Published 2019 by John Wiley & Sons Ltd.

Catchword The word printed in the direction line at the bottom of the page that indicates what the first word of the next page is. Sometimes catchwords are used only on the recto of a leaf, sometimes on both recto and verso. Differences between catchwords and the following word can sometimes indicate that changes were made during or after printing.

Chain line The impressions made by the supporting wires in a paper mould. Visible as lighter colored lines in the paper, the direction of the chain lines can help identify the format of the book. There are generally shadows around the chain line; if there are no shadows, that's a sign that it is "modern laid paper" made after the hand-press period.

Chase The iron frame in which the text and illustrations for one side of a sheet were placed, along wooden sticks and blocks known as furniture and quoins, before being locked up and printed.

Collating 1) The act of gathering together the quires in order to prepare the book for binding; 2) the process of comparing one copy of a book against another so as to note any differences.

Collation The bibliographic formula describing the ideal copy of a book in terms of format, sequence of gatherings, and number of leaves.

Composing stick The metal frame a compositor held and into which he placed the pieces of type that form the lines of text he was composing.

Compositor The person who set the type; i.e. the compositor composes the type.

Conjugate Leaves that are attached to each other because they were adjacent on the printed sheet; for example, on a quarto imposition, the first and fourth leaves are conjugate (or conjoined).

Copy 1) A single instance of a book: "I just looked at the most amazing copy of *Paradise Lost*"; 2) the source of a printed book's text: "The copy for the 1607 edition of this play came from the author's manuscript."

Countermark A type of watermark used to identify the paper mill or paper quality; usually placed on the opposite side of a sheet from the main *watermark*.

Deckle edges The edges of a sheet of paper where the deckle frame of the paper-making mould was; recognizable because of the feathery, uneven edge. The term is still used today for books in which the fore-edge is entirely uneven and rough, but that deckle edging is no longer related to the format of the book.

Direction line The line of text printed at the bottom of a page that included the catchword and signature mark; i.e. it provides direction for where the page of type is to go in the sequence of text.

Dos-à-dos A book comprised of two texts bound back-to-back, so that each text starts at the beginning of the book. Usually used for devotional texts, such as the New Testament bound with the Book of Psalms.

Duodecimo (12°, 12mo) A book format in which one sheet of paper is printed, folded, and cut to make 12 leaves.

EDIT16 *Edizioni italiane del XVI secolo*, a union catalog of editions published in Italy in the 16th century; see "Catalogs of Early Hand-press Books" in Appendix 1 for further information.

Edition All copies of a book made from (mostly) the same setting of type; see also *impression, issue,* and *state.*

Endleaves The leaves at the beginning and end of a book; part of the binding, not the text block, and therefore often different paper than the rest of the book. Sometimes called "endpapers"; see also *pastedown* and *flyleaf.*

Errata list A list of errors, and their corrections, printed in the book; from the Latin for "errors."

ESTC The English Short Title Catalogue, a union catalog of works printed before 1801 that are either entirely or partly in English or are printed in the British Isles, Colonial America, the United States, Canada, or territories governed by Britain (including false imprints claiming to be published in those regions). See "Catalogs of Early Hand-press Books" in Appendix 1 for more details.

Evans Charles Evans's *American Bibliography,* covering all books, pamphlets, and serials published in the United States from 1639 to 1820; see "Catalogs of Early Hand-press Books" in Appendix 1 for more details.

Facsimile A copy of a leaf or a book that is intended to look exactly like the original made by a range of techniques, including pen-and-ink, printed type, and photography and digital imaging. Facsimiles are usually intended as honest reproductions to assist the study of a rare book or to complete a book that is missing leaves. Sometimes, however, a facsimile can be accidentally mistaken for or deliberately presented as the original item; if it's a deliberate attempt to fool people into thinking it's the original, it would more accurately be described as a forgery.

Fingerprint A bibliographic technique for tracking variant settings of type by noticing how the signature marks or ends of lines shift; primarily a continental technique not used in Anglo-American bibliography, although it is growing in use.

Flyleaves The leaves added by the binder after the endleaves.

Font The collection of sorts that make up a complete set of type designed to work together, usually including capitols, small letters, numbers, and symbols; cf. *typeface.*

Foliation The practice of numbering the leaves (or folios) of a book, rather than the pages (pagination).

Folio (2°) 1) A book format in which one sheet of paper is printed and folded once to make two leaves; 2) a library term for books larger than a set size (around 32 cm) regardless of bibliographical format.

Fore-edge The front edges of paper in a bound book.

Format The ratio of printed leaves to sheet of paper; not the same thing as size; see, for example, *folio, quarto,* and *octavo.* Format is usually discerned by examining watermarks and chain lines.

Forme The locked-up group of typeset pages inside a chase that prints one side of a sheet of paper; the side that prints the first page of a gathering is known as the "outer forme" and the other the "inner forme."

Foxing Discoloration or staining of a page, usually a chemical reaction when poorly prepared paper ages; usually spots of a light brown or yellow.

Frisket A sheet of parchment or paper used on the printing press to mask over areas of the sheet of paper that are not to be printed.

Frontispiece An illustrated leaf facing or sometimes preceding the title page.

Furniture 1) The pieces of wood and metal used to lock up pages of type into the chase; 2) the metal bosses and centerpieces on a binding used either to protect the book or to provide decoration.

Gathering A group of leaves formed into a folded unit under a single signature; usually from a single sheet of paper but sometimes multiple sheets when they are folded one inside the other (e.g. a folio in sixes). Also referred to as a *quire.*

Gilt A thin layer of gold applied as a decorative element to bindings or to edges of the paper; usually used in combination, as in "gilt tooled" or "gilt edges."

GW *Gesamtkatalog der Wiegendrucke,* a descriptive catalog of works published before 1501; see "Catalogs of Early Hand-press Books" in Appendix 1 for more details.

Headline The line of text at the top (or "head") of a page, usually consisting of a book or book section's short title and sometimes including pagination or foliation.

Ideal copy The imaginary perfect copy of a book that is the basis for catalog records and bibliographic descriptions; the copy that you hold in your hand may differ from an ideal copy in substantial ways.

Imposition How pages of set type are arranged in a chase to create different formats; while some formats have one dominant imposition that's used, others have multiple impositions.

Impression The set of copies of an edition that were printed at the same point in time; since most hand-press books distributed their pages of type after printing, editions and impressions in this period are usually the same.

Incunabula, or **incunables** Works printed before 1501. The cut-off date of 1501 is arbitrary, but the first 50 years of printing was when printing techniques, print conventions, and the printed book trade were just being developed, and so it can be useful to see it as a discrete period.

Initials, or **initial letters** Used to refer to the decorated initial letter of a section. Such letters might be decorated by hand: rubricated (drawn in red ink), illuminated (decorated with gold leaf), or sketched in pen-and-ink. After the early incunable period, initials were often printed in woodblock, in a variety of styles: floriated (depicting flowers and plants), historiated (depicting people), or simply abstract decorations.

Intaglio (pronounced in-TAH-lio) The technique of illustration in which lines carved or etched into a plate print as black lines; the opposite of relief printing (cf. *woodblock*).

Issue A deliberately planned and identified group of copies of an edition that differ in some bibliographic way from the rest of the edition; see also *edition, state*, and *copy*.

ISTC The *Incunabula Short Title Catalogue*, a union catalog of works printed up until 1501; see "Catalogs of Early Hand-press Books" in Appendix 1 for more detail.

Leaf A piece of paper or parchment; each side of a leaf is a page: if a book is made up of eight leaves, it has 16 pages. If leaves are numbered, rather than pages, it uses *foliation*.

Ligature A piece of type with two or more letters that are joined or "tied" together, such as ff.

Made-up A copy of a book that has been made up of leaves taken from other books; also known as *perfected* or *sophisticated*.

Manuscript Anything written by hand, whether an entire document or notes in a printed work. In common usage it can refer to typed works, particularly those that an author submits for publication; when discussing the hand-press period, however, it refers only to handwriting.

Marginalia Any text that is in the margins of a work; can be printed or manuscript. It is often used as equivalent to "manuscript marginalia" but it is better to be precise in differentiating between printed and handwritten marginalia.

Metadata Data about data, such as information about what equipment was used to take an image or where a book was printed.

Mise-en-page The layout and typography of a page.

Octavo (8°, 8vo) A book format in which a sheet of paper is printed and folded three times to make eight leaves.

Offset When ink transfers to an adjacent page, usually when printed sheets are drying in heaps; today's method of offset printing works on a similar principle of ink transferring from one surface to another but is intentional, rather than accidental as in the hand-press period.

Opening The pair of pages facing each other when you open a book.

Page One side of a leaf; a work that counts by pages is paginated.

Pamphlet A short work sold stab-stitched, rather than bound. While it is a technical term related to not having a binding, it is often used as a pejorative term to suggest an ephemeral and unimportant text.

Parchment The skin of a sheep used for binding or manuscripts; often (but incorrectly) used interchangeably with *vellum*.

Pastedowns The endleaves pasted to the boards at the front and end of a book; part of the binding, not the text block.

Perfecting 1) In printing, finishing the second side of a sheet of paper; 2) in collecting, the process by which owners add leaves to a copy of a book to replace missing or damaged leaves.

Printer Used to mean either the person who physically printed the book or the person who caused the book to be printed (today we would refer to this second role as the publisher). The two roles could be done by the same person or by different people.

Publisher The person who caused the book to be printed by supplying the money and the paper and the text. In the hand-press period, this was not a term used, and this person was often referred to as the printer.

Quarto (4°, 4to) 1) A book format in which a sheet of paper is printed and folded twice to make four leaves; 2) a library term for books of a certain size (usually 32 cm or less) regardless of bibliographic format.

Quire A group of leaves that are folded together to make up a single unit signed with the same mark; a quire is often one sheet of paper folded, but it may also be multiple sheets folded inside each other, as in a folio in sixes. Also known as a *gathering*.

Recto The top or "right" side of a leaf; in this book, the recto is top side of the leaf on your right; in a stack of loose leafs, the recto would be the side you read first; see also *verso*.

Register 1) To line the paper up with the type so that the text and images print where they are intended to; 2) the lines of letters at the back of a book that identify the order of the gatherings.

Rubrication Using red ink to add decoration to a text, usually as a way of calling attention to important words or to the beginning of a section of text; from the Latin word for "red." Ink decorations in other colors (blue and purple are fairly common) are often referred to as rubrication or as pen-and-ink work.

Ruled Of a page, 1) having inked borders created by using straight lines of metal; 2) having manuscript lines (often red) drawn to create borders or underneath the lines of text.

Sammelband (pl. sammelbände) A group of separately issued books that have been bound together into a single volume; from the German for "bound together" and sometimes referred to instead as "bound withs."

Signature The mark at the bottom of the recto side of a leaf that helps ensure that leaves are gathered in the correct order. The signature C3, for instance, indicates the third leaf in the C gathering. The recto side of a leaf is indicated with an "r" and the verso side with a "v": C2v faces C3r in an opening.

Skeleton The parts of a forme that are reused from one page setting to the next, usually consisting of the headline and the wooden furniture used to hold the imposed pages of type in place.

Sophisticated A copy of a book that has had leaves from other copies or facsimile leaves added in order to make it complete. See, also, the second usage of *perfecting*.

Sort The pieces of type that represent a single typographical mark; a single glyph (A, %, ff) is a sort.

Stab-stitched A book that has had its gatherings stitched together by stab-sewing near the gutter but has not been sewn into boards or other covering material.

State The copies in an edition with bibliographical variants, such as stop-press changes, or cancels; since different sheets might or might not have stop-press changes, a copy might be in an uncorrected state for one variant but a corrected state for another.

Stationer Anyone involved in the book trades; could refer to either printer or bookseller.

STC The *Short-Title Catalogue*, a print union catalog of books printed between 1475 and 1640 in the British Isles and North America or in English in other parts of the world; now subsumed into the ESTC. See "Catalogs of Early Hand-press Books" in Appendix 1 for more detail.

STCN *Short Title Catalogue, Netherlands*, a union catalog of works published in the Netherlands between 1540 and 1800; see "Catalogs of Early Hand-press Books" in Appendix 1 for more detail.

STCV *Short Title Catalogus Vlaanderen*, a union catalog of works published in Flanders before 1801; see "Catalogs of Early Hand-press Books" in Appendix 1 for more detail.

Text block 1) The part of a book that comprises the leaves of text and illustrations; separate from the binding and endleaves; 2) sometimes used in discussing typography or mise-en-page to refer to the part of the page that is comprised of the main block of text, as opposed to margins or gutters.

Tipped in A leaf that has been added to a book by pasting it to an adjacent leaf near the gutter, as opposed to sewing it in; e.g. a cancel leaf, or a leaf added by a later owner.

Tooled, tooling The lines and decorations that are pressed into leather bindings; bindings can be gilt tooled, in which the tooling has gilt added to its marks, or blind tooled, with no additional coloring or gilding.

Turn-ins The portion of material covering a board that is left visible over the pastedown. Turn-ins are sometimes signed by the binder with a stamp.

Tympan The part of the printing press on which the paper to be printed is placed.

Typeface A group of fonts all of the same style, but usually in different sizes; Times New Roman, for example, is a typeface (cf. *font*).

Uncut When a book's edges have not been trimmed while being bound; an uncut gathering will have leaves with deckle edges; not the same as *unopened*.

Union catalog A catalog that brings together the catalogs of a number of institutions; most of the catalogs discussed in this book are union catalogs.

Unopened When a book's leaves have not been cut after folding; this is sometimes referred to as the bolts having not been split. If a quarto is unopened, the first and second leaves are still connected at the top, as are the third and fourth leaves.

USTC *Universal Short Title Catalogue*, a union catalog of works printed in Europe up through 1650; see "Catalogs of Early Hand-press Books" in Appendix 1 for more detail.

VD 16/17/18 *Verzeichnis der im deutschen Sprachbereich erschienenen Drucke*; the three German bibliographies of 16th, 17th, and 18th century editions published in German-speaking regions; see "Catalogs of Early Hand-press Books" in Appendix 1 for more detail.

Vellum Skin from a calf used in binding or for manuscripts; often (but incorrectly) used interchangeably with *parchment.*

Verso The "reverse" side of a leaf; in other words, the back of a "recto." It is tempting, but incorrect, to think of "verso" as being "left." While the page on the left of an opening might indeed be the verso of a leaf (if the text is a left-to-right language, like English), it is not the verso of the leaf it is facing.

Watermark The impression left by the wire figure on the paper mould; it often denotes the paper size or quality. It may be accompanied on the opposite side of the mould by a *countermark* identifying the papermaker.

Wing Donald Wing's *Short-Title Catalogue of Books Printed in England, Scotland, Ireland, Wales, and British America, and of English Books Printed in Other Countries, 1641–1700*; now incorporated into ESTC. See "Catalogs of Early Hand-press Books" in Appendix 1 for more detail.

Wire line, or **laid line** The impression left by the laid wires that make up a paper mould; they run perpendicular and are set closer together than chain lines.

Woodblock 1) An illustration printed by carving out white space from a block of wood, leaving the lines standing in relief to print black; 2) the piece of wood used to print such an illustration.

Index

The index covers the main text, illustrations (shown in italics), and the two appendices. Locations in Appendix 1: "Further Reading" are in bold and appear primarily in the main heading for each entry; if there are relevant readings for subheadings outside of what is provided in the main term, those are added. Terms in Appendix 2: "Glossary" are indicated by a dagger (†) following the main term; a page number is not provided for the location in the glossary, but it is organized alphabetically and immediately precedes the index. Not all terms in the glossary are in the index, so if you don't see a term here, you might wish to check there as well.

Studying Early Printed Books 1450–1800: A Practical Guide, First Edition. Sarah Werner.